MW00908553

The
TEAM

PAUL BABCOCK

Copyright © 2019 Paul Babcock
All rights reserved
First Edition

PAGE PUBLISHING, INC.
New York, NY

First originally published by Page Publishing, Inc. 2019

ISBN 978-1-64462-811-9 (Paperback)
ISBN 978-1-64462-812-6 (Digital)

Printed in the United States of America

""The Team" Quotes

"I had the privilege of playing for Coach Gordie Gillespie, then working with him at the University of St. Francis for twenty-five years. You will have the opportunity to meet this extraordinary man and coach in Paul Babcock's outstanding book. I can assure you that this will be the most worthwhile read. I had the opportunity to direct basketball clinics for Medalist Sports Education and the USA coaches throughout the country. This provided me with the chance to meet some of the best basketball coaches in America--John Wooden, Dean Smith, Bob Knight, among others. Gordie would not take a back seat to any of them. How can any coach have his basketball, football, and baseball teams win a combined 2,402 games and be inducted into 19 Halls of Fame? And these are just two of the many accomplishments in his incredible career. Paul's book will enlighten you on one of the greatest coaches in the history of American sport. Enjoy the read!"

Pat Sullivan- Retired Athletic Director and
Basketball Coach at University of St. Francis

"I met Gordie when I was a young kid and he inspired me to play football for Joliet Catholic High school, the best football team in the area. From the day I got there, he changed the rest of my life. I thought I was a fullback and he said, 'No, Son, you are an offensive lineman.' From that moment on, Notre Dame to the Chicago Bears, it was Gordie's decision.

Tom Thayer- 1985 Super Bowl Champion- Chicago Bears- current color commentary WBBM Radio broadcast of the Chicago Bears

"Success is not measured in wealth, it is in the heart of the man who has been told 'you cannot,' and then he stands and walks boldly forward."

Joan Gillespie- Wife of Coach Gillespie

"I am pleased that Paul wrote this book so people could see what an amazing Coach and man Gordie was. I admired him as a young man, and he was always a gentleman who wanted the best for his athletes and stressed the importance of school and teamwork."

Mark Grant- Former MLB pitcher and current TV color commentary for the San Diego Padres

"I had the great fortune to know Gordie Gillespie in a way few others have had. Without question the greatest coach and teacher ever to come from Illinois. Gordie Gillespie was my basketball and baseball coach, my mentor, my colleague, and my friend. He taught me respect, humility, and hard work while recognizing my potential to be more that I thought I could be. I am sure that thousands of other "Gordie disciples" could say the same thing. When Gordie entered eternity, his flame was not extinguished, but rather can be seen in all of us who have been touched by the only coach in our hearts. He was the best of the best."

Tom Kennedy- former President of New Ventures of Regis University Denver, Colorado

"Coach Gillespie made a profound impact on me when I played for him at Joliet Catholic. I used to say that I played three positions at JC. I played guard, tackle, and end. I sat at the end of the bench, guarded the water bucket, and tackled anyone who came near it. I never played much in the games, but I loved the game and my teammates. Coach Gillespie saw something in me and encouraged me to coach. To this day, I am so grateful for his guidance, friendship, and for being my mentor."

Dan Sharp- Joliet Catholic Academy Athletic Director, Former Head Football coach

"Gordie Gillespie was the greatest coach in the history of baseball, but he wasn't just about the game. He knew it like nobody else, but he was so much more than that. He was a father figure when I had none. A role model when I needed one the most. A guiding force at a time when my life lacked direction. A disciplinarian with an endless motive of love and respect. An encourager. A leader in the greatest sense of the word. As a former Major League Baseball Player, husband & father, businessman, etc., I still hold many of his lessons deep in my heart and apply them still. I'm not half the man I am today without Gordie, and I believe there are countless who would share that opinion. Rest in peace, dear friend. Your imprint on this world will echo throughout the ages."

Les Norman- Host of syndicated sports radio talk show "Breakin' the Norm" Kansas City, Mo., Former MLB player

"Paul captures the essence of St. Francis baseball. The TEAM is what is important. A great clubhouse can empower you to play beyond your normal abilities. As a motivator and coach, Gordie Gillespie stands alone!"

Steve Parris- MLB pitcher 1995-2003, St. Francis Graduate

Dedication

I would like to dedicate this book to my brothers and sisters. In the last few months, they have shown me real strength and determination. Our mother's dementia has become much worse since our father, her husband of 68 years, passed away in June. The patience and care that they have given her is something of which my father would be extremely proud. Their heart and dedication is not uncommon, but this basic act of human kindness and decency is too often overlooked. Human beings can make a positive impact on the people around them by simply choosing to love. I am proud of their example.

Contents

Acknowledgements

This book was possible because of all the people who contributed in one way or another. My biggest supporter has always been my wife, Christie. She provided great insight from the very beginning of this project. My daughter, Grace was my first editor. It was no surprise to me that she earned a full academic scholarship to Ball State University.

It was a great pleasure for me to reminisce with all my college teammates who added great stories to the book. Our former Sports Information Director who became the Athletic Director, Dave Laketa clarified and verified so much information that I could never thank him enough. Ed Soldan and Alex Fernandez provided valuable insight that only close friends can do. I also appreciated the open and honest feedback from my former assistant coaches and friends, Dan Galligan and Tim Herbert.

Pat Leonard was one of the first non-family members to whom I entrusted my work. He skillfully provided tips that improved this book tremendously. Coach Tony Delgado and I spent hours on the phone making sure that this could be the best version it could possibly be. He was also the person who inspired me to write the book. Joan Gillespie, Gordie's wife, was the first person who really made me believe that this was a well written book. I will be eternally grateful for that gift. I cannot thank Pat Sullivan enough for all the guidance he has given me.

Chapter 1

The Farm

I grew up on a two-hundred-acre farm in Northern Illinois. It was only a twenty-minute ride north to the Wisconsin border and the town of Clinton. We would have to drive thirty minutes to the west to reach the thriving metropolis of Rockford, Illinois. We raised a variety of crops that were rotated every few years. The most common crops were corn, alfalfa, oats, and wheat. They were all used in some capacity to help with the animals that we raised. There was not a lot of traffic since my nearest neighbor lived a quarter mile away from me. In fact, the closest town was about three miles away and had a population of only eight hundred people. In college, my friends jokingly stated that most of the population of Poplar Grove was our family of twelve, plus the Black Angus cattle and swine that we raised. We were so remote that I can remember the whole family canning fruits and vegetables. My older siblings could always tell when the cows were grazing again in the spring. They claimed that they could taste the grass in the milk. Now that is country.

My parents, Richard and Lorraine, raised ten children. They had five boys and five girls who were born over the course of twenty-one years. We had a lot of fun making people name us and put us in order. The correct order is Chuck, Patti, Dick, Kathy, Louise, Phil, Pete, Terri, Judy, and Paul. My parents were in their forties when I was born. Since I was the youngest, I would tell people my parents

13

quit when they finally got it right. There was such a big age gap between Chuck and me that I do not remember a lot about him. One of my only childhood memories of him was on the day he packed up his ugly brown paisley 1970s van and moved out to Colorado. He became a steelworker and lived with our cousin Ray. I did not really even know who he was until my sister Louise "Weez" drove my sister Judy and me out to see him on a summer vacation. My parents were pretty brave to allow their twenty-one-year-old daughter to drive their seven- and ten-year-olds across the country during her week-long vacation from her job at Sundstrand. I remember complaining a lot about headaches when we were out there. I am not sure if they were caused by the elevation, but they were a daily occurrence. One of the days when I whined about a migraine, Chuck growled, "You are a headache." It is safe to say that we did not like each other very much at that time of our lives.

My sisters Patti and Kathy as well as my brother Dick were all in college when I was born. My oldest sister, Patti, actually transferred to Northern Illinois University so she could commute and help my mom a little. She also needed to save the money that would have been spent on room and board. I guess there was a rumor going around town that Patti was my mom. My earliest memory of her was when she took me to the grocery store. As we were walking in, a driver of a Hostess truck asked me if I wanted a snack. I think he was trying to impress my sister. I acted very shy because he was a stranger. My sister encouraged me to get into the truck with her, and he invited me to take anything that my heart desired. I picked one Twinkie. He tried to get me to take a whole box, but I was contented with one. I guess my parents had already taught me the difference between *want* and *need*—a lesson that is imperative if you have ten children.

My siblings who impacted me the most were the ones who were still living at home while I was growing up. I spent a lot of time with my sister Judy since she was born only three years before me. My sister Terri was seven years older than I was, and she excelled a little more in academics than athletics. I was more interested in the latter from an early age, so I gravitated more toward my brothers. Pete and Phil were involved in all high school sports. I loved action and wanted to be on the move. I had so much energy that my siblings would describe me to other people as "hyperactive." I didn't know what that meant, but it sure didn't sound like a compliment.

We were so remote that my hyperactivity actually endangered my life one summer day. I was a typical kid who loved to ride my bike as soon as I mastered the skill. Most of the time I would ride around on our driveway, which was only partially paved. The portion that led to the barn and shed was a gravel path. I loved building up speed on the paved area and then hitting the brakes when I reached the gravel. My back tire would slide and kick rocks away from my bike when I slammed on the brakes. I felt like a real stuntman. Occasionally, I wanted to see just how fast I could go. This meant that I would have to start in the garage and head toward the road. My parents made it very clear that the street was off-limits unless an adult was with me. I guess I decided to ignore this rule since I hardly ever saw any traffic. As I left the driveway, I glanced to the right and saw our neighbor's truck approaching quickly. The vehicle was so close that it was even with our mailbox. When I hit the middle of the road, I turned my handlebars and leaned to the left as hard as I could. The grill of the truck was close enough to touch but, by the grace of God, never made contact with me. I am sure Mrs. Johnson was more scared than I was. She stopped and talked to my parents about the incident. It took some time for them to let me ride my bike again.

Playing outside was my favorite activity since I had so much space to entertain myself. My mom would always say, "How about you read a book?" My response was always the same: "I'm going out to play." I spent hours on end running around doing whatever my imagination led me to experience. Some days were spent in the hayloft, others exploring the "woods." I was superactive, and as long as I checked in for meals and came in when it got dark, I was allowed to go anywhere on the property that I wished.

The farmhouse was over one hundred years old. When I was very young, we even had an outhouse that was still standing on the property. It was out back by the clothesline, the rhubarb patch, and the grapevine. The house was so old and drafty that before winter hit, we would stack straw bales around the house and staple plastic over the windows. The creepiest place in the house was the basement. This is where we stored all the produce that we canned. Anything that grew in the garden that couldn't be eaten before it expired was preserved until we could eat it later; nothing went to waste.

I didn't like being in the basement because of the musty smell. It was always dark and damp down there. It seemed like, more often than not, I was the one sent down to fetch whatever was needed. As the youngest, I was the gopher—go for this and go for that. I always felt like there was some monster waiting to jump out at me, so I tried to make the trip as fast as possible. I made sure that I knew where everything was located so the creatures couldn't get me. I figured that if I was in and out fast enough; there was no way that they could get me. I didn't complain as much when my family sent me down to the freezer because that meant that we were having ice cream for dessert. Besides the freezer, my favorite item was the washing machine that was probably from the 1950s. The tub with the agitator was pretty standard, but the top of the machine had two rollers designed to squeeze the water out of the clothes. I often imagined how bad it would hurt to put my arm or even my whole body through it. This was an important feature since we didn't have a dryer. My mom would hang the clothes on the line outback even in the winter. It amazed me that clothes could be frozen stiff and be dry when they unfroze. When I got older, a coach dropped me off after practice and commented that the "yellow" underwear on the line must be mine. Being the youngest helped me identify when someone was just teasing me. I learned how to take a joke early in life.

The outside buildings were a lot less scary. We had a two-story grainery that had several compartments to play in. It was really fun when we stored corn in there for the cows. It was like having a big sandbox made of corn kernels. The shed was located right next to the grainery. This was where we stored all the machinery. It was a huge steel building that was tall and wide enough to store three combines side by side if we needed it. My dad made sure to put up a basketball hoop so we could practice, but I preferred playing in the combine and on other equipment. My family normally left the doors slightly open because they were so big that I could not budge them by myself. If it was raining, I could normally be found in there or the barn.

The barn was only a few paces away from the other buildings. The lower level provided shelter for the animals. We had several stalls for all the swine. A portion of the building housed the steers that were fattening up for slaughter. There was an additional outdoor shelter for the cows and calves. My favorite part of the barn was the hayloft. By the middle of summer, it was nearly filled with hay. I loved climbing up and down the seemingly endless stacks. When it was stacked high enough, I could walk on the support beams that were about six inches wide and eight feet off the ground. It was like having my own balance beam within a giant jungle gym. There were plenty of nooks and crannies to hide in as well. There was plenty to do in all that space.

No matter where I went, I was running. I remember trying to see how fast I could get from one place to another. I was convinced that new shoes always made me faster. When I got my first pair of Zips, I set all sorts of personal records. Even the name of those shoes implied speed. I had no need for a stopwatch; monitoring my speed in my head was as accurate as I needed. My dreamworld seemed very realistic. It was close to a mile from one edge of our property to the other. I loved to run by the creek that ran through the pasture. My agility developed pretty quickly, dodging all the land mines that the cattle left behind. If there were tons of cow pies, I would hope that the manure was already dried by the sun. The pasture led to the wooded area of the land, which was also filled with obstacles that I had to dodge. The vegetation between the trees could be quite hazardous. There were plenty of thistles and plants with thorns that would rip open my skin. I would run through the woods as fast as I could while trying to avoid getting scratched to pieces. Little did I know that my "training" would be very useful in my career in sports and on the farm.

Different crops and pastureland for the cows surrounded the buildings. We ran an electric fence along each piece of pasture so the cows would not get into the crops. From time to time, we would discover that the cows had gotten out of the pasture because the electric fence was broken or had a "short" in it. One summer day was very vivid in my memory. My sisters Louise, Terri, Judy, and I were corralling the cows. The directions were very clearly spelled out to me: remain calm and quiet and stay in your position, slowly directing the cattle toward the spot where they got out. If they got spooked and started running, chances were slim that we would catch them quickly. More than likely, they would separate, and it would take hours to get them back in the pen. Sure enough, a calf tripped on a rock and startled the rest of the herd. I was alongside them on the right when they started to run. I knew I could not let them turn right into the field in front of us, so I took off. My shoes were not on very tight, and they flew off within the first few steps. That did not slow me down whatsoever. I was able to keep up with them until they slowed down. My sisters were well behind. Luckily, the cows went right where they were supposed to go. I got the credit, but I am sure I had little impact on the outcome. "Wow, you can really run," my sisters told me. It was a great thrill to hear those words. It was affirmation that I was good at something that I spent a lot of time doing. My speed came in handy more often than I would have liked because the cows seemed to get out often.

Luckily, I had family members who would entertain me from time to time. I really don't remember my sister Kathy before she was with Charlie Balmes. I was still very young when she was in college, and that is when she met him. There was one particular moment, when I followed them into the woods, the event made me sure that I would always like him. They got there just ahead of me and hid up in a tree. They made bird noises to give me hints to try to find them. I would giggle as I searched for them because I knew they were nearby, but I could not locate them. After about ten minutes, they could not contain their laughter, as I stood right underneath them completely baffled to their whereabouts.

Charlie spent a lot of time with me inventing new sports of some sort. My favorites normally involved the garage. When I was small, he would just throw a ball up on the roof and see if I could catch it when it came off. He challenged me by making me stand in a place where I could not see the ball until it rolled off the edge. My reactions would have to be quick as soon as it appeared. Sometimes I could hear it coming, which helped my response time. Occasionally, the ball would get caught in the gutter and he would lift me above his head so I could retrieve it. Once I got it, he would weave back and forth like a drunken sailor and pretend that he was going to drop me. He knew how to keep me entertained. When the car was not inside, we would pretend to be goalies and one person had to kick, hit, or throw some type of ball past the other. He would adjust the rules to make the game competitive, but it was obvious that if I wanted to win, I would have to earn it. I remember laughing the whole time because of how fun he would make it. The winning shot was superdramatic and celebrated like it was the championship in a professional league.

Very rarely did we play a conventional sport. I think he wanted to make it seem more like play than practice. For example, if I wanted him to pitch to me, it would turn into a game of who could throw it past the other person more. If his pitch hit the side of the garage five times, it was his turn to hit and I had to throw it past him. I always looked forward to Charlie coming over because he would surprise me with something new. One time he woke me up on an early Saturday morning and asked if I wanted to go for a run around the block. I had no idea what that meant, but I said yes because I would be hanging out with him. The run was between three and five miles long because we actually ran the only thing in the country that was shaped like a city block. We took the country road into Poplar Grove and then circled back on another country road. In the middle of the run, he introduced me to his "Turbo Boost." Without saying a word, he sprinted ahead as he simultaneously and loudly passed gas. It sounded and appeared that he was being thrust forward by his flatulence. He always made any activity fun and instilled a love of being active within me. It was too bad that he was not always around when it was time for chores.

My siblings teased my parents that they had so many children so the chores would be completed more quickly. We definitely learned how to work without complaining. My grandfather taught my dad that people who know how to work will always have a job. That lesson was passed on to all his children for sure. As a little kid, I tagged along with my dad and did any little task that he needed. Most of the time, it dealt with moving the cows to a new pasture or helping mend the electric fence. It is hard to forget the first time my dad said, "Go ahead, grab it." The jolt wasn't as bad as my reaction, but the look on my dad's face was so memorable. He had a sparkle in his eye and a smirk on his face that clearly told me I had been tricked. It was clear that he liked to play as much as work. I like to think I picked up his sense of humor and devious ways.

Being the youngest of ten children had its advantages. I learned very quickly what acceptable behavior was and what was not. I was born into a conservative Irish Catholic family. The nine siblings are normally a dead giveaway. My parents were strict, but it was very clear that it was for our own benefit. My four brothers and five sisters would always say to me, "You are spoiled rotten." I just told them that I was the favorite because I learned to avoid all their mistakes. I will admit that my parents were more relaxed when I was growing up. It was probably that they were getting older. I know that one of my biggest goals in life was to not disappoint them or cause them any real headaches. I wanted them to be proud of who I was. My dad always stressed that I was representing the Babcock family name, and I took a lot of pride in that from my earliest times.

There was no question what we were doing on Sunday morning. We would all pile into the Chrysler Monaco and head to church. Somehow, we all managed to fit because we had big bench seats. The bigger kids had to sit the smaller kids on their laps. It is a good thing we were never in an accident because there were definitely not enough seat belts. I am sure it looked like a clown car emptying when we got to St. James in Belvidere. We filled an entire pew with our clan.

Every once in a while, Dad would surprise us with a trip to Donut Depot if our behavior was outstanding in mass. My parents did not always talk about how we should act, but they always showed us. Their expectations were clearly reflected by their Catholic values. The golden rule was king in our home: "Always treat other people as you wish to be treated; if you are mistreated, turn the other cheek and forgive them for their trespasses." It was clear that there was never a good time to lie, cheat, or steal. They were the models of consistency. If I was not paying attention or was misbehaving in mass, it only took a disappointing look from either of my parents to correct my behavior. If I was a slow learner, they would squeeze my arm to get my attention. The pressure that they applied to my arm was sufficient to help me act in the proper manner.

If we made mistakes, we were expected to take full responsibility for our actions. They both made it very clear that if we got in trouble in school, the punishment would be far worse when we returned home. Under no conditions would they believe our word over an adult's. It was also crystal clear that this was done out of love. It was part of a process that would help all their children contribute to society in a positive manner.

From time to time, my parents had to deal with a few "incidents." The fire trucks had to come because my brother Dick set a portion of our property on fire and it got out of control. Pete and Phil were close to being "Irish twins" (born within twelve months of each other) and caused their share of trouble with their partner in crime. I was told stories of how they nearly burned the house down by playing with matches under the porch. When they were older, they put the truck on its side by driving too fast. It is a measure of how much they feared our father that they were able to push it back up onto its wheels by themselves. The expectations were not always met, but the lessons were learned.

As all of us got older, our responsibilities changed. Like all kids, I couldn't wait to do the things that my older brothers were doing. At the same time, when the moment I was asked to do something new came, I realized how terrifying it was. When I was seven years old, my dad decided that I was old enough to drive the lawn mower. I am sure his only qualifications were that I could touch the pedals. He seemed to ignore the fact that my legs were not strong enough to push the break. I remember telling my dad this and he simply replied, "If you need to stop, you'll muster the strength." He was right, as usual, though one time I ran right into the biggest tree on our property. My dad just came over, backed me up, and sent me on my way again. Looking back on this now, I think he was just trying to show me how much he believed in me and wanted me to know that I could accomplish more than I might expect. My "on-the-job training" taught me a lot about facing my fears too.

My mom taught us a lot about working as well. She knew that half of life was just showing up and the other half was working once you got there. She was proud of how many times her children had perfect attendance in school. I actually went about five years without missing a day. There were a few times that I should have missed, but my mom made me go to school unless I had a temperature over 102 degrees. She must not have cared too much about getting other children sick, but it sure taught me to have mental and physical toughness.

As an adult, I remember events that seemed insignificant at the time, but when they came flushing back, I realized how much I really learned. My brother Phil literally taught me the hard way that you have to get back on a horse if it bucks you off. He was very close to taming his horse, Teardrop. She was appropriately named due to the shape of the white patch of hair on her forehead. Phil thought it would be a good idea if he would put me on Teardrop's back as he led her by the bridle down the blacktop road. It sounded good to me until I realized he was not going to use a saddle and her mane was the only thing that I had to hold on to. Something scared Teardrop, and I fell right on the back of my head on the street. My head was throbbing instantly. All I wanted to do was walk the last few hundred yards back to the house. Looking back on it now, Phil was probably just covering his butt. I am sure he figured the longer I stayed with him, the more I would calm down and our parents would not find out. He insisted that I stop crying and get back on. I refused because he didn't control the horse the first time. He simply got down to my eye level and said, "If you don't get back on this horse, you will regret it the rest of your life." I didn't know exactly what he meant, but I was pretty sure it was about being persistent and sticking to something until the job is done. You can't stop shy of your goals. This painful event was just one in a series of things that would eventually turn a little boy into a man.

My journey to manhood revolved around my chores on the farm. Typically, I would feed the cows grain once in the morning and once at night. There were four buckets, each one of them held five gallons of corn. I would carry them about one hundred yards and dump them in the trough in the pen. I would then have to climb the ladder into the hayloft and drop a few bales of hay into the feeding pen. These daily chores became easier the older I became. I always viewed my rite of passage on one particular chore that occurred three times a summer: bailing hay!

There were always three "cuts" of hay. We would get fewer bales of hay each time because the alfalfa would not grow back as thick. The first time the hay was "cut" down was in early June. It would have to dry a day or two before it was raked into a row, and then it would dry another portion of a day. All this had to be carefully planned out because rain could really ruin the quality of the hay. There were a variety of different jobs, and I ranked each one of them according to how tough they would make me. My older brothers always set the standard for where I wanted to be.

I ranked driving the tractor the lowest. That did not always mean that it was the easiest. In fact, this was where I had the greatest probability of being yelled at. The driver's first priority was to make sure the *entire* row of hay was picked up by the bailer. The tractor pulled the bailer, which was offset slightly to the right. The wagon was hooked up to the back of the bailer, which created a long line of equipment. Scraps that were left behind would have to be picked up by the bailer at the end of the day, which would waste diesel fuel. Not leaving scraps behind was most difficult to accomplish on the corners. When the tractor was traveling clockwise, the trick was to take a wide turn, but the strategy was quite different when going counterclockwise. The tractor would actually need to run over the row of hay for a short period of time before returning it to just inside the row. Unfortunately, turning the steering wheel too sharply would cause the wagon and the bailer to collide, and turning too wide could keep the bales out of the reach of my brothers on the wagon. I failed to mention that this also required the driver to look back and forth between the front and back of the tractor. I was about eleven years old when I was expected to pick this up. My training session was a couple of trips around the field. Listening and following directions were paramount on the farm.

As I got older, bigger, and stronger, I graduated to more physical jobs that fit my personality better. The easiest jobs were unloading the wagon. This was a two-person job. Initially, I was placed on the top of the hay wagon where I would roll bales down to Judy, Terri, Kathy, Weez, or whoever else who would signal when they were ready. This job was fun because rolling a heavy object at your older siblings is always fun. However, I didn't enjoy it because it wasn't intense enough for me. I wanted jobs that would make me into a strong athlete. A step in the right direction was the other unloading position. This required more strength because I had to brace myself for the impact of the bale rolling down the hay wagon and then pick it up and put it into the conveyor belt that carried the bale to the hayloft.

The real action was in the hayloft. This job was probably the most challenging because after the bale dropped off the conveyor belt, I would have to carry it to the back of the barn and stack it tight so we could fit all the wagonloads of the year. Another detriment of improper stacking would be stepping between the bales up to your thigh. Ending up with shaft in your socks is no treat; plus, my jeans would get pushed up, and my legs were scratched up. In general, the stacking strategy would involve laying a base layer. This would become tricky when the bales were placed all the way to the landing zone. My brothers and I would have to set the bale before the next one would land on our heads. Once the foundation was laid, levels of bales were gradually stacked higher and higher. This became like doing a stair master while carrying a forty- to eighty-pound weight. This was made even more uncomfortable due to the fact that the barn was stifling hot because air did not circulate with the lack of windows. That did not stop us from talking a little trash early in the day when we had a lot of energy. Occasionally, we would tease the people on the wagon that we were bored and needed them to unload faster. Typically, there would only be about four bales on the "elevator" at a time. That was thrown out the window as soon as the smack talk began. The family members unloading the wagon would add as many bales as they could. This continued until the bales were touching from end to end on the conveyor belt. Once we opened our big mouths, there was no going back. It was an unwritten rule that no matter what, we would never ask them to slow down. Luckily, we were smart enough to only run our mouths when the wagon was nearly empty. We were pretty sure we could keep up with the intensity for a short period of time.

On a typical day, we knew the wagon was getting close to empty when there was a longer gap between bales. Our job was officially complete when the conveyor belt stopped and we heard the tractor go silent. Then there was a mad dash to the water hose. We had our own well with a hydrant that brought up the freshest water. In addition to quenching our thirst, we would use it to cool off and remove the hay from our arms. We would actually rinse out empty milk jugs the day before and fill them a little more than halfway and put them in the freezer. These frozen gallons of water would be a big part of my favorite job: loading the wagon.

These blocks of ice would either ride on the tractor with the driver, be stored in the bailer with the twine, or sometimes ride right alongside us on the wagon. Regardless, they would melt fairly quickly in the sun. There was nothing more refreshing than that ice-cold water. Keep in mind that we did not stop for water breaks. There was work to be done so we had to strategize when we could get water. Sometimes that required us to wait until the wagon was full.

Graduating to loading the wagon was a big step. It was as challenging as the hayloft, but one advantage was that I got to be out in the fresh air. The hayloft might shield me from the sun, but I wanted to be outside and, hopefully, have a breeze. There were many challenges to loading, but each of them brought a great sense of achievement. Every brother wanted to be able to brag about how many bales they fit on a wagon. For some reason, I remember 181 bales being very difficult to beat. There was virtually no way to get to that magic number if a solid foundation was not set with tightly packed bales. Every layer that was laid must be placed in a different pattern in order to "tie" the wagon together. If bales were stacked properly, they would hold the others in place. The wagon would naturally rock back and forth because the field was not perfectly flat. A small load might only have five layers, whereas a huge load could have as many as eight. The biggest disgrace would be if some bales or a whole section fell off the wagon as it was being taken from the field to the barn. Not only did this create more work, but the poor loader would never hear the end of it. My dad would often decide when there was enough on a wagon, especially if we had some recent spills. Every once in a while, he would let us go for it.

Most times there would be two people on the wagon. Normally, my brothers would be doing this job, but from time to time, they could be paired up with one of my sisters. There were a few different methods that were used. Many times we would alternate taking the bale out of the bailer and stacking it at the back of the wagon. Sometimes one person would take the bale out and toss it back to a designated stacker. This person would be showing the process to the person tossing. This way, everyone would eventually know how to stack. Sometimes it was necessary to have the strongest person on the wagon tossing the bales. As the wagon filled, there was not enough room on the front of the wagon. One person had to be stationed on top of the bales. Sometimes tossing bales required the worker to throw the bale over their head. The other worker would grab it and put it into place. A few times when I was small, I was actually a third person on the wagon who got to place the very last bales at the top. It felt like I was a hundred feet off the ground. The biggest thrill, however, came when I was much older and was finally able to load an entire wagon by myself. I remember relishing the hard work. The tougher the job, the happier I was. I was growing physically but even more into the person I was meant to be.

There were plenty of jobs that I did not look forward to on the farm. Many of the jobs centered on our other animals: pigs. I don't think the number of pigs we had ever came close to the number of cattle on the farm. At one point, we exceeded over one hundred Black Angus cattle. I would guess we never had more than seventy swine at one time, even when the sows gave birth to piglets and a large litter could yield up to sixteen. One of my earliest memories with hogs dealt with them giving birth.

Even though it was a cold winter night, the chill was eliminated by a space heater in the barn and a heat lamp in the pen. We had a sow that was struggling through the birthing process, so it was important to be there in case help was needed. This was going to be the first time I got to witness an animal being born. I thought they would just shoot right out, but I actually watched my brother Pete use a tool to pull a piglet from her mother. I am sure it would not be that much different from an obstetrician using forceps, but that is a pretty disturbing sight, even for a farm boy. Little did I know that this so-called miracle of life was about to make me more than just a spectator. Since this sow struggled so much throughout the entire labor, it was hard to tell if she was done giving birth even though there were ten healthy piglets. Pete decided that he wanted to know for sure if the ordeal was over. He looked at me and said, "I need you to check and see if she has any more babies in there." I responded as any eight-year-old would, "How do I do that?" He looked at me with a grin and said, "Stick your arm in there and feel around." With a dumbfounded look, I replied, "Whaaaaaat?" He proceeded to guilt me into doing it by explaining that I was just the right size and if I didn't, there was a good chance that any remaining piglets would die. The next thing I knew, I was shoulder deep in this hog without a clue to what I was doing. Pete continued to instruct me to just reach around as much as I could. The only way I could describe what I felt would be to reference the movie *Ghostbusters*. It was like sticking my arm into the ghost that slimed Bill Murray. All I felt was slime. No more babies for me to rescue. It was an experience I would never forget; luckily, I never had to repeat it.

I am relatively certain that during the next summer, I discovered firsthand what "Rocky Mountain Oysters" were. Experiences on the farm seem normal until you share them with your friends that live in town. I learned very quickly which kids found my stories cool and which ones found them disgusting. I was never repulsed by what I was doing, but one time my brother's friend grossed me out. Pete told me that he had a friend coming over to help us castrate the male pigs. He called him "the hillbilly," and I was about to find out why. The two of us would catch the pig and pin it to the ground. I used my hands to keep his front feet still and my shoulder to pin his head to the ground. He used a similar method on the back half of the animal. Pete had an extremely sharp knife, a bucket, and a bottle of diesel fuel. Once the animal was secured and barely moving, Pete would quickly preform the "surgery." A quick two-inch incision was made, and the testicles would pop out. I should have worn earplugs because the squeal was immediate and seemed loud enough to shatter glass. I remember thinking, *Poor little guy, I wouldn't want someone doing this to me either.* Once the testicles were exposed, it was a quick slice of the connective tissue. He then threw the extracted material into the bucket and doused the open wound with diesel fuel (this helped prevent infection). Then it was on to the next victim until the job was complete. When we finished, my brother thanked his friend but was greeted with a more enthusiastic "Thank you" as the "hillbilly" grabbed the bucket of removed testicles. As he drove away, my brother explained that to some people, these are a delicacy. When I shot him a confused look, he went on to explain that he was going to cook them and eat them. I decided right then and there to stick to bacon.

There were times that my family raised swine, but by the time I was about eleven years old, we would only go and buy young (about two months old) pigs that my sister Judy and I would eventually show at the Boone County fair. My dad would normally buy four "Chester Whites," two for me and two for Judy. This was so we could each have a "Pen of Barrows." Dad made it clear that if we wanted to get these pigs truly ready for the fair, we would have to work every day. We bought the pigs in the spring, and the fair was the first week of August, so we spent most of the summer doing something with them on a daily basis.

You would think that the basic expectation would be to feed and water the pigs each day. My dad knew that if we wanted to have champion pigs, an extra effort would be necessary. Every day before the heat of an Illinois summer would set in, my sister and I would walk our pigs. No, we did not have leashes. We would let them out of the pen and let them walk around our yard, which was about five acres of grass. The main chore was to keep them from heading toward the fields. Initially, we just chased them around because they were very wild. We didn't need to chase them for long because they tired out quickly. My dad realized that walking the pigs would have several positive outcomes. Each day that we walked them, they became calmer and would be more familiar with us. They would also have better muscle tone than the pigs that they were competing against.

Once every few weeks, my dad would require us to wash the pigs. When we finished walking them, we would force them into a fenced-in area on the clean concrete next to our water hydrant. The first time we washed them was always the hardest because they were not accustomed to it and were more resistant. In addition, they were caked in filth. Swine love to wallow in their own waste. Luckily, the hose was strong and removed most of the material. In order to make sure that everything was removed, we would scrub them with a brush and a bucket of soapy water. Once they dried off in the sun, we would "oil" their skin to make sure they did not dry out and it would give their coat a nice shine. The more often we did this chore, the more comfortable the pigs became with us and the cleaner they were when it was time to go to the fair. These jobs really taught me a valuable lesson about working every day toward a goal and eventually it will pay off. Sometimes the payoff is what you get, but most times, it is really what you become.

There were several payoffs the first time I showed a pig in the ring. I could tell that most kids had not been working with their pigs because they took off running. My sister and I had pigs that we could control and keep in front of the judge. The more time a pig spent around the judge, the better chance we had at receiving an award, which led to money in our pockets. More times than not in my 4-H career, I won an award with my pigs. The various awards ranged from grand champion barrow to reserve champion pen of barrows. My favorite award was for showmanship.

I remember before I was old enough to join 4-H, my dad would take me to hog shows. Part of the reason was that many of his childhood friends were judges, but the other reason was to prepare me for showing pigs. My dad would always point out who he thought was doing the best job showing their pigs and why he thought that. More times than not, those kids would win the showmanship award and their pigs would win as well. I made the connection that if you want to be successful, you only have to mirror what successful people are doing. I put it into practice and was able to win the showmanship award on a couple of occasions. My dad always let me keep the money that I won even though he purchased the pigs, their food, and the entry fees. The only requirement was that I put the funds into the bank. The money I made helped pay for my college education. That was enough motivation for me to pay attention and follow the example of successful people in any area that I wanted to pursue.

Judy and me "measuring" the corn for my dad

It was a tradition to take a picture by the corn
on July 4 to see how high it was.

Family portrait seventies style

My brother Dick didn't let the horse buck me off.

Showmanship award winner

Chapter 2

Baseball

Without a doubt, the way my parents raised me on the farm determined who I am today, but the game of baseball unexpectedly became the vehicle that would steer most of my decisions. I remember very clearly the first time organized baseball was introduced to me. I was playing in a tree with a friend from church. Jimmy Gates lived in Belvidere, in my mind a major city, but in reality, it was just a small town known for the Chrysler plant. Jimmy loved all the space we had and accompanied me on many adventures. We were in the middle of climbing the biggest tree in our front yard when a strange car pulled into the driveway. It was only strange because I did not recognize it. Very few cars ever passed by my house, but when they did, I waved because more than likely, it was a neighbor. I remember what happened next as if it were yesterday. It was insignificant to me at the time, but looking back, it was a simple moment that changed my life.

I saw my dad come out of the garage to greet this man as he got out of his car. A handshake and a few short pleasantries were exchanged. A few moments later, my father shouted, "Paul, do you want to play baseball this year?" My response was immediate. "Nope." I was five. I was so wrapped up in the make-believe world that Jimmy and I had created that there was no way I wanted anything to take me away from that. All I knew was that he wanted to know if I wanted to play baseball right then, and at that time I was perfectly content to be hanging from a tree. Little did I know that baseball was not going to interfere with my plans for that day. The man was at my house because the league needed more players to make an even number of players on about three teams. I am sure he knew about the Babcocks and their ten kids. Well, luckily for me, my dad ignored me and told the guy quietly that I would love to play. When my dad told me that a few days later, I was confused because I remembered my answer. My dad looked at me and said, "You *will* have fun." My father's words were law in our house, so I knew not to complain. In retrospect, the choice he made for me changed my life; from that point on, I chose baseball.

The first year I played Little League baseball, it was a pretty typical experience. As a little kid, I was just happy to be outside with kids my age. I remember my mom repeatedly asking me if I liked baseball. I always responded, "No, I *love* it." I think she asked because I was slightly younger than many of the other kids and I spent some time on the bench. I liked kicking my legs back and forth and making channels in the dirt with my feet. The strange thing was that I even enjoyed just sitting there and watching. My dad dropped me off at a game one time on his way to Chrysler before working a twelve-hour shift. As he put the car in reverse, he looked at me and said, "I wish I could stay and watch your game, I love watching you play." At that time, I am sure I responded with, "No big deal." However, I spent a lot of time thinking about that simple phrase as I grew up. It showed me how much my parents loved me and how hard they needed to work to provide a nice life for me. I saw plenty of kids that never had someone in the stands watching them because they didn't care about sports or their kids. I was lucky because I had parents that cared about both.

I spent a great deal of time at my brothers' games when they were in high school. I don't remember a lot about baseball because there were several times when a female friend of Pete or Phil would entertain me on a picnic blanket. They would comment on how cute I was, so I thought they were my girlfriends. I do remember that Pete was a catcher because he had a crazy mitt that was jet-black with florescent orange trim. My brother explained that it helped the pitcher focus in on the glove more. I picked up a few tips when the ladies weren't distracting me.

When my team didn't have a game or practice, I created my own games of baseball. The first game I played was one-on-one baseball. This involved my sister Judy, who was three years older than I was. She loved sports as much as I did, so I normally had a competitor in anything we came up with. Unfortunately, most of the games we created took place near my parents' bedroom. My dad made a baseball field about fifty feet from the house. The backstop was made with four telephone poles and chain-link fencing. Each of the bases was from a piece of machinery called the "Disc." It was similar to a plow, but it broke the dirt down into smaller chunks. The round disks were approximately the same size as a base. The outfield fence was the natural boundary of the cow pasture. The only problem with the fence was that the top was strung with barbed wire. An additional problem with the field was that we had two apple trees in right field. That really only created an obstacle when my brother Phil came up. He was the only lefty in the entire family.

My dad worked the third shift at the Chrysler plant in Belvidere. He would work from 10:00 p.m. to 6:00 a.m. then come home and sleep from 6:30 a.m. to 10:00 a.m. That is when he would get up and work the farm. He would work the fields until dinnertime and then take another nap until he had to leave for work. My sister and I knew that many days, we would have to help with odd jobs that Dad needed done. This meant that we had to play while we could, and that was while he slept. I am not sure how much he slept because we were typical siblings who had to argue about everything. "That's not fair," "You're a cheater," "I'm never playing with you again" were daily phrases that I know he heard us shouting. I know this because every once in a while, we would hear him shout "I'm trying to sleep!" or "Can't you two ever get along?" He would even remind us before we started, but it never made a difference. We got so caught up in the competition that nothing else registered.

I know that he didn't like hearing us fight, but I am sure he loved the fact that we were playing sports. He loved sports, and it was clear that he enjoyed that we had a similar passion. Every so often, someone would tell the story about Dad missing the birth of my sister Kathy because he was playing in a softball game. It was very clear that he loved to play himself. He even modeled this by making sure every holiday or family reunion would not end before playing a softball game. We always had more than enough players for two teams when all our cousins were over. Everyone, and I mean everyone, played. It was a tradition that the oldest two members of the family would be the captains and pick the teams. They would always start with the youngest person and say "I *want* —— on my team." The youngest person would have a huge smile because they were picked first and must be the best. When I was young, it took me a few years to figure out the best players were picked last. The captains always made the teams fair. We modified the rules so no one was sitting on the bench. There were times that we had fifteen defenders spread across the diamond. The batting order was always in the order that you were picked. If a child wasn't strong enough to swing a bat, an adult would help them. If a really strong player came to the plate, a smaller child would be positioned next to an adult for protection. We definitely kept score and wanted to win, but deep down, we all knew that it was about being together and having fun. I always looked forward to those huge family gatherings, but I knew most of the time, it would just be Judy and me.

One-on-one baseball followed the same simple rules of baseball with a few exceptions. The "pitcher's hand" was out if you were not on a bag. It was important to make a good decision if an extra base hit occurred. If the pitcher got to the ball before you were safely at second, third, or home, you were out. We had to make up that rule because the balls were too hard for "pegging" the opponent before they reach the bag. Most of our arguments occurred over safe or out calls. Once you reached the bag safely, the "ghost" runner would take over. That was the simple premise of the game.

Since my sister was older, she had the advantage in strength. I really had to develop my speed and my pitching in order to keep it close. If I gave her too good of a pitch, there was no doubt it would go for extra bases. I would sometimes run a little slower so she would get greedy and go for an extra base. That is when I would turn on the jets. I am sure she would do the same thing when I was hitting. We developed a great rivalry and played on a regular basis. As the years rolled by, I remember being frustrated that people would comment on how good of an athlete my sister was and they didn't include me in that category.

Once in a while, my parents would allow us to have friends over to play. We only invited kids who would want to play sports. We would always divide teams evenly by age, so my friend was on Judy's team and vice versa. After one game, my sister made a comment about my friend on her team. She said, "I hope you become as good as him someday." I didn't let her know it, but I was furious on the inside. I repeated phrases like that over and over again to myself. I wanted to be better than those people around me, and these comments were all the motivation that I needed. I decided the only way people would make those comments about me was, if I worked harder than everyone else did. I learned to love competition, and I discovered that I hated losing more than I loved winning.

When my sister wasn't around or didn't want to play with me, I had to entertain myself. I would play this game thousands of times throughout my childhood. I would throw a tennis ball against the silo and catch the ricochet. That was it, over and over and over again. It might not sound fun, but it was amazing the amount of nail-biting bottom of the ninth games that I generated. The game was so fun because of the design and placement of the silo.

The silo was located next to the barn and a large open stretch of grass about the size of a Little League baseball field. The silo was made of concrete blocks that were fitted together with a tongue and groove pattern. Steel rods that went around the circumference of the silo also fastened them together. These rods were spaced out about every three feet all the way to the pinnacle, which was around fifty feet high. These obstacles are what really created a game within the game.

Many times the tennis ball would strike the flat surface of the concrete blocks and return routinely to my glove for an easy out. I could alter what kind of play it was, depending on how high or low I threw it off the silo. If I threw it near the bottom, I would be working on ground balls. If my throws were elevated, the ball would stay in the air longer. However, as a youngster, my throws were quite erratic and would hit the support rods at different angles. Balls that would hit on the top of these rods would turn into sky-high infield pop-ups or deep fly balls, depending on the velocity that the ball left my hand. When a ball hit the middle of the rod, it created a sharply hit line drive. If the ball hit the bottom portion of the rod, the reaction normally leads to a high bouncing ground ball. My favorite play was created when the ball hit the objects that connected the rods together. These connectors were oddly shaped and produced ricochets that were unpredictable. Many times it would cause the ball to shoot to the "gap." You can imagine the different game scenarios that were created with all these possibilities.

I can still hear my mom yelling from the kitchen, "Paul, come in for supper!" Many times, I would try to get a few more outs because I was probably in the middle of an inning. However, my parents were very traditional; they wanted everyone to eat as a family while the food was hot, so most times I would have to remember the number of outs and where the base runners were located. We would eat all three meals together as a family, and everyone started with saying grace. My parents would also utilize this time to communicate. We were all expected to share part of our day with the family, and "It was fine" was not satisfactory. The discussions were part of our routine. Many times my interest was piqued because we were discussing something sports related. Trying to eat quickly so I could get back to my game was not an option. I had to be excused from the table. Normally, that meant that everyone was finished eating and the conversations had ended. This was one area where my dad was a little more lenient with me. When I got the word, I was right back to my game.

Out of the corner of my eye, I would sometimes catch my parents watching me from the kitchen window. I wondered what they were talking about as they watched. I am sure that didn't last for long because I played for hours and hours. As soon as I ended one game, I would start up another. In fact, I only stopped when it got too dark to see. No matter how many games I played, I was playing for the

Chicago Cubs. My dad grew up on a farm in southern Wisconsin, so he was a Milwaukee Braves fan. When the team moved to Atlanta, he needed another team, and the proximity of Wrigley Field fit the bill.

Sometimes I would imagine that I was my favorite player. You would think that he would play for the Cubs, but that wasn't the case. In the early 1980s, "my guy" became Andy Van Slyke of the St. Louis Cardinals and the Pittsburgh Pirates. I am sure I chose him because he was on WGN several times a year against the Cubs. I liked that he seemed like a regular ballplayer who got things done with hustle and hard work. Recreating his style of play was a daily event courtesy of "silo ball."

There was one key problem with this game. When a tennis ball hits a baseball glove, it does not respond the same way as a baseball. The weight of a baseball will cause the glove to naturally close. On the contrary, it was important to watch the tennis ball into the glove and use hand-eye coordination to secure the catch. Squeezing the glove tightly and using two hands was also beneficial. I had no idea that the silo ball was teaching me the fundamentals of the game.

I have a very vivid memory of one particular play that occurred at the most dramatic point of my imaginary game. The Cubs were playing in game 7 of the World Series in Wrigley Field. Their opponent was the neighbor to the north, the Milwaukee Brewers. They were in the American League at that time and were known as Harvey's Wall Bangers. My first MLB game was in old County Stadium in Milwaukee. I tagged along with my brother-in-law Charlie Balmes and his friends. I was in awe of the Milwaukee lineup because I witnessed Bernie the Brewer going down the slide after several home runs on that warm summer night. As a kid, everything seemed so huge and magical. The stadium and the amount of fans were overwhelming. I definitely was experiencing some sensory overload. Hearing the odd calls of the vendors and the free exchange of money with their patrons was quite the experience. However, nothing was larger than life than the players.

I can still remember most of the names that Charlie wrote on his lineup card that evening. Scratched out in pencil were names like Simmons, Oglivie, Cooper, Thomas, Yount, and Molitor. These players left a huge impression on me that night. The sweet swing of lefty Cecil Cooper was the first to christen the seats that night. Stormin' Gorman Thomas soon followed his example. Home runs tend to leave a mark on a young man's brain. My favorite part of the night was when a Jackson Five song came over the loudspeaker. "Rockin' Robin" was the song that was played as future Hall of Famer strode to the plate. The crowd was so electric that I actually got goose bumps trying to figure it all out. It was fun to learn a little more about each player throughout the game. Charlie talked about each player as they were hitting and pointed them out when they were in their position on defense. I tried to watch him keep score, but the game moved so fast. That taught me that those people who called baseball boring had obviously never tried to keep score. From that point on, if I was going to root for an American League team, it was going to be the "Brew Crew." Everything about that night was fun, even their nicknames. I am sure that is why they became a common opponent in my "Silo series."

I can't remember their exact batting order, but Stormin' Gorman Thomas, Cecil Cooper, Robin Yount, and Paul Molitor got the majority of at bats in my decisive game 7. Why bat nine when your favorites can hit over and over again? It was the bottom of the ninth, and the Cubs were clinging to a one-run lead. The bags were jammed full of Brewers, and there were two outs. Up to bat was the cleanup hitter "Rockin' Robin" Yount. I watched enough games to know some of the stats of the best players. In my mind, it created a little more drama. On the year, Yount knocked in 114. His RBI total was only second on the team to Cecil Cooper, who had 121 that year. Yount led the team with a 0.331 batting average. It was only fitting that he would come to the plate with the game on the line. This situation would be the toughest of his career, after all, he was facing Paul Babcock, and I literally played every position! As I released the tennis ball, I could tell it was headed toward one of the connections. As an athlete, it is always important to anticipate what is about to happen. The ball hit off the top left corner of this oddly shaped connector. It shot toward the gap in left center field, and I was off to the races. I became oblivious to the precarious point in the game and focused on my one objective: *catch that ball!* My speed helped me get close to the falling projectile, but it appeared that I would come up short since it was sinking fast. Out of instinct, I left my feet and dove as far as I could. Unfortunately, this was right at the edge of where the grass ended and the gravel driveway began. Fortunately, I earned a temporary wound that I could show my family for the most spectacular catch that I have ever made. I repeated over and over: Cubs win, Cubs, win, Cubs win the World Series. They were World Series champions all because of a game-winning catch by the hero in left field, Paul Babcock. In my mind, those were real events that transpired and nothing could take away from my excitement. The adrenaline rush of that perfect situation is what kept me coming back for more. It also helped me completely ignore that my forearm was all torn up. The motto of the US military was in full effect, "Pain is temporary, and pride is forever."

Chapter 3

Maitland

M y main goal in Little League was to play for McClay Grain, our town's only Pony League team. The coach was a local citizen named John Maitland. Everyone in town knew John. It was not because our town was so small either, but that didn't hurt. He was in charge of the public works. Most days you could be sure to find him at the sewer plant or fixing something in Poplar Grove. Actually, there was a good chance you could find him in about ten minutes by simply driving down our main street or one of the few side streets.

He lived just down the road from my grade school and right across the street from my friend Mark's house. John was still a bachelor who lived with his mom and her identical twin sister. Occasionally, I would see him washing his car when I walked to Mark's after school. John had two cars that all young kids loved, a Z28 and a Jeep Wrangler soft top. Most summer days he would be driving around town with the doors and top off the vehicle. If I couldn't find him, I could ask anyone I saw outside. They would normally say, "I just saw his Jeep parked…" To be perfectly honest, I normally checked the parking spots outside Zink's Tavern on my way to his house. John enjoyed the occasional adult beverage.

John was a character. He was always smiling, laughing, and telling jokes. No matter whom he talked to, he would tell a new joke which would inspire the person to respond with the most recent joke that they had heard. I cannot think of a time that I spent with him where I did not laugh multiple times. He was easy to get to know because he would talk about the things that he was interested in. Part of the reason I liked him so much was because we shared a common interest in sports. We didn't always see eye to eye, but we definitely shared an interest in our professional football team.

We both loved the Green Bay Packers. Poplar Grove was only a twenty-minute drive from the Wisconsin border. In fact, the Packers played half of their home games in Milwaukee County Stadium, and that was under a two-hour drive for us. That was about the same distance as Soldier Field. Proximity was not the reason for our devotion to this team. We loved the Packers because of the rich tradition and the legendary Coach Vince Lombardi. John was able to experience the Packers under Coach Lombardi. My childhood was ingrained with stories of the past. We admired him because of *how* and *what* he taught his players. It was about doing things the right way. If you were ten minutes early, you were already five minutes late. He believed in discipline and hard work. Lombardi told his players that if they pursued perfection, they would catch excellence. If they executed the fundamentals over and over, they would be very difficult to beat. His players were devoted to him not only for the championships that they won but for the men that they became by playing for him. I looked for these character traits in all my coaches. I, in turn, wanted to become someone of whom my coaches would be proud as well.

John and my dad would tell me stories about how Lombardi molded the Packers into a great team. This, of course, was followed by stories of some of their favorite individuals. They would preach about the toughness of Ray Nitschke and the talent of Paul Hornung. I heard about the "Ice Bowl" when they defeated the Cowboys on the famous Bart Starr QB sneak. Hanging in my house, there was actually a picture of Bart Starr standing between my brothers Pete and Phil when they were about eleven and twelve years old. I couldn't help but become a Packer backer. The other professional team that I grew to love did not have such a rich tradition.

I became a Cub fan because my dad would tell me everything about his favorite players. One day he told me that the Cubs traded their best player. I made a bunch of guesses before he told me: Rick Reuschel. I just laughed because I didn't think he looked like an athlete. My dad assured me that he was one of the top pitchers in the league and great players come in all shapes and sizes. I found that to be exactly true as my fandom grew.

I enjoyed watching Jay Johnstone because he was so entertaining. He was known for his classic wit and keeping other players loose. Once during a rain delay, they showed him wearing clown shoes and diving through the water on the field tarp. Even though he was great at making people laugh, he took the game seriously and was a great competitor. The first Cub player that I followed closely was Bill Buckner. I knew he was a tough guy because he played through injuries and hobbled around the field. He was a great hitter that always seemed to be in the middle of the Cub's offensive action. I was a little heartbroken when he left for Boston, but the year he left, I became a full-fledged Cub fan. The 1984 season was magical and filled with a colorful cast of characters.

Initially, all great nicknames captivated me. We had Ryno, Bull, Penguin, Red Baron, and the Sarge. They would have been harder to remember if it wasn't for their performances on the field. The Cub's announcer, Harry Caray, made them larger than life. Harry became an icon in Chicago by singing the seventh-inning stretch at Wrigley Field and making Bud Light commercials. Cub fans appreciated his love of the Cubs and less-than-perfect delivery. It was clear from the start that his partner, Steve Stone, was the brains of the operation. Harry had a real enthusiasm for the team and created a fun atmosphere. When the Cub's power-hitting catcher came to the plate, he would sing a special song in tribute to number 7, Jody Davis. He made me love the top of the lineup when he nicknamed them the "Daily Double." This was because Bob Denier and Ryne "Ryno" Sandberg were consistently on base. Ron Cey seemed to waddle around the bases after a home run, so he was dubbed the "Penguin." Leon "Bull" Durham, Gary "Sarge" Matthews, and Kieth Moreland added to the offensive machine. The highlight of the summer might have been when the hated Cardinals came to town and Ryne Sandberg became a legend by homering twice off the great relief pitcher, Bruce Sutter.

The Cubs had a closer of their own named Lee Smith. I was excited to see if he could strike out the side in the ninth with his great fastball.

John did not share my love of the Chicago Cubs. In fact, he rooted for one of their archenemies, the New York Mets. Whereas I was raised on stories of the demise of the '69 Cubs, most people remember that season for the Miracle Mets. Cubs fans remember a lead slowly fading in September and an ominous black cat. We commiserate over the misfortunes of our favorite players, like sweet-swinging Billy Williams, Ron Santo, Fergie Jenkins, and Mr. Cub "Let's Play Two" Ernie Banks. It was a shame that Jack Brickhouse never announced a World Series winner for my dad.

John found humor in the misery of Cub fans. My heart was broken officially for the first time when the '84 Cubs went into San Diego with a two-game lead and missed the World Series because they lost three straight to the Padres. I will never forget hanging up in the sewer plant was a newspaper with the headline "Cubs Blow Big One." John howled at that every time a Cub fan came to see him.

John related to most people because of his sense of humor, but he had a serious side as well. He was passionate about the American Civil War. Every time I visited his basement, all his artifacts and memorabilia amazed me. His walls were all decorated with pictures of his favorite generals. It was simple decision for him because he believed that the Northern generals were foolish. He preferred Southern leaders like Lee and Stonewall Jackson. I believe he equated them to coaches. If you are smarter than the other guy, you will win a lot of battles that you originally shouldn't have.

His bookcases were filled with different books on the period, and his tables were covered with maps of battlefields. Leaning against the wall were a variety of rifles and swords. Strewn along the windowsill were dozens and dozens of lead bullets. It was his own personnel museum. The extent of his collection was on display when he finally moved into his own home, expanded by the fact that every year he would take a trip with a friend to visit a different battle site. He was sure to bring home something significant to add to his assortment. He always planned his trips around his number one passion: baseball. The Pony League season normally wrapped up near the end of

July. By that time, he had already trained someone to manage the town while he was gone.

John coached for as long as I can remember. I couldn't wait to play for him. He treated every moment as a teachable moment. When he passed out the uniforms, he actually took the time to show us the proper way to put them on. Our uniforms were similar to the Oakland As with the exception that we had blue where their green would be. John started with our socks; we had to make sure that they were pulled tight up to our knees with no wrinkles. I am sure he stole the no wrinkles idea from Coach Wooden at UCLA. He knew that those wrinkles would lead to blisters, which would decrease performance. Attention to detail was key to executing his plans. Our stirrups were next in line. It was important to align it with the arch of our foot so it would not slide out of our cleats. I will never forget when he showed us the proper way to put on our pants. Initially, I thought that he was joking. We were required to turn our pants inside out and pull the leg holes up to our knees. We would then grab the belt line and pull them up. We were shocked that this method created a perfect fold at the top of our calf muscles. This old-school look was the only option for us. John said that wearing the uniform pants down at the ankles looked like pajamas and we wouldn't be sleeping. John communicated the importance of all catchers and infielders wearing an athletic supporter and cup. He did not want his players being afraid of being hit below the belt. Every player was also required to wear the same color sleeves under their jersey. The final piece to looking like a team was for everyone to bend the bill of our cap and have them facing forward. He taught us to look great *and* play great. We always took a great deal of pride in the way we looked. Looking like a ballplayer was important, but not as crucial as preforming like one.

We loved the challenge of playing in tournaments with different age levels. Most of the time, we played in tournaments with bases placed at eighty feet. That was always done because longer throws would be difficult for young players to make. I was actually more than seven months younger than most of the people in my grade. I would joke with my friends that my parents just wanted their hyperactive tenth child out of the house. I clearly remember our first tournament with ninety-foot bases. I was playing third base, and it felt like the majority of the balls came to me. I made every play. Balls hit right at me, slow rollers, a backhanded play down the line, and I even started a double play after diving on a smash to my left. The funny thing was that, that was my shortest throw of the day and I threw it too low, but the second baseman caught it out of the dirt and sent it on to first. At one point, I actually heard a disgruntled hitter yell out, "That third baseman is killing us!" It was one of my proudest moments.

I later found out that John and his assistant coach quietly discussed the issue before the game. They were not sure that I could handle the long throw from third because I was so used to the shorter bases. I remember being disappointed that they doubted me. It was like I was continually reminded to keep working if I was going to impress people. At the end-of-the-year party, I got a plaque that said, "Most Improved." I did not let it show, but that put a chip on my shoulder that would never leave. If they gave me this award as a compliment now, did that mean they thought I was weak at the beginning? I wanted to prove to people that I was good enough if I was just given a chance. It turned out to be a great motivator because I wanted to prove to my coaches that I was a quality player.

John prepared us by practicing the fundamentals on a daily basis. If we ever complained, he would tell us that it was nothing compared to what he had to do in the army. The only real comparison to the Army was that he was very organized. There wasn't a part of the game that we didn't work on. If it could happen in a game, we spent time on it. Practices were intense. We covered different drills every ten to fifteen minutes. Skill development was a priority to coach Maitland. Practices were so productive because time was not wasted. However, if you were to ask players what their favorite part of practice was, the answer would be unanimous…trick plays.

Part of the reason we loved the game of baseball so much was because of how interesting he made it. We had to play close attention since we never knew when he would try something unusual in a game. If an opponent had a base runner on third and you heard Coach yell out "Ninety," you would see our pitcher throw an intentional wild pitch. The pitcher had to hit a general area on the backstop that John had discovered would ricochet the ball right back to the catcher. As soon as the pitcher released the ball, he would rush to cover the plate. The timing was always perfect. The base runner would arrive at the plate just after the ball arrived for an easy out. Coach was smart enough to never run that play against a team twice. My favorite verbal call came when we were on offense. The call "Sixty after two" meant that we had base runners on second and third. Whenever strike two was called on the hitter, the base runner on second would steal sixty feet toward third. The entire dugout and coach would scream and yell to get back. The runner would put both hands on his helmet like he had made a terrible mistake and would start to retreat toward second base. The catcher would see this and throw behind the runner to second. Unbeknownst to the catcher, the base runner at third would be cheating off the bag and would take off for home as soon as the catcher released the ball. His throw and the return throw were never fast enough to get the runner at home, and everyone would be safe. Those were just a few of the ways John outcoached other teams.

John also found ways to make a home-field advantage an actual thing. He would giggle as he rolled a ball from home down the third baseline. He could even start the ball six inches foul, and it would always come back fair. The field was sculpted to help our fast runners reach first on most bunts. Players were encouraged to play small ball, but at the same time, our defenders were urged to get the ball as quickly as possible, preferably in foul ground.

There was one specific play that John was especially fond of running. He loved the suicide squeeze. If it was executed perfectly, it was nearly impossible to defend. When our team ran it, the other team rarely even got an out. As soon as the pitcher started his delivery, the runner on third was stealing home. Coach trusted that the hitter would get the bunt down and the run would score easily. Unfortunately, there was one occasion where the worst possible scenario reared its ugly head, and I just so happened to be the batter. We were playing a rival team from the town of Sharon that had not beaten us in about the last twenty games. I remember John telling us later that the Sharon coach had told him that he had finally figured out that when John tugs on his ear, the suicide is on. John acted like he was disappointed that he figured it out when, in actuality, that was not the sign.

We were down one run in the bottom of the seventh with one out and a runner on third as yours truly strode to the plate. I got the sign and was prepared to tie the game up. As the pitcher released the ball, I could see out of the corner of my eye that my teammate got a great jump. I calmly squared my body at the exact same time. The pitch was at the top of the strike zone. I stabbed at the ball and bunted it in the *air*, right back to the pitcher. He easily caught it and tossed to third for a game-ending double play. If I had missed the ball, the runner might have scored, gotten back to third, or even gotten out of a rundown. If I could have just fouled it off, we would still have an opportunity to tie it up some other way. For the first time in my life, I felt like I had let everyone down. It was not something that I ever wanted to experience again. I wanted to do anything that I could to help my team become successful. Failing my team was heartbreaking.

Coach Maitland also wanted us to understand the game. He would literally test our knowledge with a written exam about the game of baseball. Most of his questions dealt with the basic details and situations of the game. He also liked to infuse his humor into the test. One of the questions read, "Who played first in Abbott and Costello's routine?" All of the players had no idea and made ridiculous guesses. We were enlightened when he went over the answers and explained that "Who's on first" is a famous comedy routine.

My dad was John's home plate umpire for several years. He knew John's tendencies and was always in the right position to make an accurate call. It is a testament to how much he loved sports that he would spend his very fleeting free time doing this. My dad would not allow John to pay him; it was a small way that he gave back to the community. I am sure that a benefit to the job was having a great spot to witness a game that his sons were playing. Dad made it very clear to any of his sons who would play for this team that during the game, he was "Sir" or "Blue." We also knew that he would call the game as he saw it and there would be no favoritism. In fact, we knew to be swinging at anything close with two strikes because we would be rung up like any other player.

I think John loved my dad as an umpire because he called the pitches at the knees or slightly below. He was very consistent and called it the same way for both teams. John knew that we had great infielders, and low strikes meant many ground ball outs. Our pitchers knew to pound the bottom of the zone. It would keep all the defenders on their toes because there was a good chance that they would get many opportunities to make a play. Our games would fly by because balls were not flying into the gaps. John taught his teams that *this* is the way the game is supposed to be played.

In the three years that I played for John, we had a ton of success. Our losses never reached the double digits even though we would play in some tournaments with kids a year older than us. The summers were filled with caravanning with buddies to a nearby town. All the parents got along very well and would even alternate driving so their sons could be together even more. We never wanted the season to end, but when it did, we had a team party. Each year, someone different would host. The best parties always involved some sort of water sports.

My parents decided to host one year, and we had a blast. We did not have a pool, but we *did* have a pond. It was located just past our wooded area on the farm, pooling in the shape of a V. About fifty yards long in each direction and twenty yards wide, our pond could be as deep as fifteen feet but as shallow as a few feet at the beaches. The highlight of the day came when we started a mud fight by scooping up the silt at the bottom of the pond. The water went from being crystal clear to being very murky. Luckily, my parents didn't care because they knew the dirt would settle again.

I remember John asking my parents and the parents of two of my teammates if he could take us to a clinic in the off-season. He wanted to take us into Joliet to the College of St. Francis. This was the school where Coach Gordie Gillespie and his assistants Tony Delgado and Joe Heinsen called home. Over the years, John had spent a lot of time learning the finer points of the game from these coaches. In fact, John would tell us stories of the speeches that Coach

Gillespie would give at clinics that he was attending. He loved the enthusiasm that he possessed in each presentation. He claimed that once during a presentation, Coach Gillespie got down on all fours and somehow related how the same toughness in football could be utilized in baseball. John would also repeat one of his favorite quotes from Coach about players taking so long getting loose before practice: "A dog doesn't stretch before chasing a car" or "People don't stretch before running out of a burning building." Gordie was well-known nationally for his knowledge of the game, his success on the field, and his youthful exuberance. Coach Gillespie was in his late fifties when Coach Maitland first saw him speak. If John heard that Coach Gillespie was speaking at a clinic in a nearby state, he would gladly drive the several hours to hear him. He never said this, but I am sure he reminded him of Coach Lombardi. John was hoping the three of us could learn some more about baseball and, hopefully, be inspired to continue playing far into the future.

I will never forget the first time I met Coach Delgado. John introduced me, and Coach Delgado continued to shake my hand for what seemed to be five minutes. During that whole time, he asked me questions about myself and my team. He left quite an impression on me. I was then introduced to Coach Gillespie. He made me feel like I was the only person on earth. His handshake and eye contact sent a message that his attention was completely focused on *me*. I had never experienced anything like it. The man that I had heard so many stories about took the time to make me feel special. It was unmistakable why John admired him so much. He had a certain personality that drew people in. Even though I had just met him, I felt like he would do anything for me and that would cause me to do the same for him. I don't remember anything else about our visit except that, right then and there, I decided to go to CSF to play baseball for those "old coaches." It was a big decision for a kid still in junior high. The excitement of that possibility kept my mind occupied the whole ride home. That thought even distracted me from the fact that riding in the back of a Z28 for two hours is uncomfortable even for a five-foot-nothing teenager. Suddenly, the cool factor of that car dropped dramatically.

Bart Starr with my brothers Phil (left) & Pete (right)

My dad in action behind the plate

John Maitland is on the far right. McClay grain was no longer the sponsor by the time I was in seventh grade. American Legion Post 205.

Chapter 4

High School

At the end of my eighth-grade year, my parents had a new home built on our property in the woods. Designed to be energy efficient, half of the house was buried in the side of the hill. This natural "insulation" enabled the house to stay cooler in the summer and warmer in the winter. It was perfect because we could walk right out our front door during the first snowfall and go sledding. We would have to be careful, though, because the pond was at the bottom of the hill. When the sleds packed down the snow enough, we would run the risk of sliding too close to the water. If the pond was not frozen solid, we would bail out of the sled near the bottom.

Since my father loved sports so much, my mom let him build a baseball field with a backstop. This field was unique because it was now on an island. My dad expanded the pond and turned it into what looked like a giant moat. The water was about thirty feet wide and in the shape of a circle. He created a covered bridge that was made of large shipping containers that were welded together. The makeshift bridge was so heavy that it had to be lifted into place by a large crane. My dad's imagination allowed him to create his own little paradise. This location was enjoyed by just about anybody that we knew. My dad loved to share his play land with anyone who was interested. All my family members invited countless people over to marvel at this outdoor wonderland.

My sister Judy and I were superexcited to move into the new house because my parents had a satellite dish installed. At the farmhouse, we only got the channels that the antennae on the roof picked up. The dish literally received hundreds of channels. We could watch nearly any movie that we desired. Until this point, if we wanted to watch a movie, we would have to go to the theater with our sister Weez. We spent a ton of time with her because she was fun and loved the movies. She enjoyed them so much that she got a subscription to HBO. Sometimes we would spend the weekend so we could have movie-athon. She only lived fifteen minutes away, so our parents didn't mind that we spent so much time with her. One night, she took me to her friend's house for dinner. I remember eating hamburgers because they were the worst that I ever had. Weez was furious with me because I made some remark about how bad the meat tasted. She tried to cover for me by explaining that I had never eaten ground beef from the store; I had only eaten the fresh beef directly from our farm. The couple just laughed it off but probably thought that I was a brat.

After dinner, they sat around talking as I played. I eventually wandered into the living room to find her husband watching HBO. I said, "What are you watching?" He responded, "*Rocky*." I walked in right at the point when Rocky was kissing Adrian for the first time. I made a weird noise, covered my eyes, and turned to leave the room. He told me that the scene was almost over and I would love it if I give it a chance. I sat down, and within a few minutes, I was mesmerized. I loved the general theme of never giving up and being determined to accomplish your goal. My favorite parts were easy to identify. I was so inspired when he told Adrian that he couldn't beat Apollo but he wanted to go the distance to prove to himself that he wasn't just another bum from the neighborhood. I actually had to fight back tears in the fourteenth round when Rocky got knocked down and his trainer Mickey told him to stay down. I jumped up and down when he got up and asked for more and Apollo shook his head in disbelief.

After the movie ended, he asked me if I had seen the other two. When I shot a confused look at him, he explained that I must be living under a rock because there were three *Rocky* movies and plans for a fourth. I couldn't wait to see them all because I was already hooked. I even started doing tons of sit-ups and push-ups. Eventually, I mastered the one-armed push-ups. I would like to think those workouts got me ready for high school sports.

After three great years playing for John Maitland, it was time to progress to the next natural step, North Boone High School. Three grade schools filtered into North Boone. I knew most of the kids from Manchester and Capron grade schools because I had been competing against them in junior high basketball or competing with them in junior tackle or on McClay grain. I was confident that we would continue to have success at this next level. Let's just say we didn't quite achieve what I was hoping we would.

Our mascot was the Vikings, and not just because we were a small group of villagers. Much to my dismay, our village was about to shrink. One of our best athletes moved to Florida with his family. Two more players moved to another school nearby because they felt the academic and athletic programs were much stronger. That might have been true, but I felt betrayed. In my eyes, we would have been more successful if they had stuck with us. I know there were other factors, but each season did not go as planned.

I would love to say that I was a terrific three-sport athlete, but since I attended a small school, it was much easier to make the team and play. I really didn't have a favorite sport. I was passionate about whichever one I was currently playing. The fall was always reserved for football, and most red-blooded Americans would have a hard time accurately explaining the thrill of Friday night lights. I remember barely watching my brothers play when I was a kid because my friends and I had our own pickup games in the shadows of the stadium. I did see my brother Phil catch a punt at his shoe tops going full speed. That taught me to play hard and give my full effort; if you screw up, at least you gave it everything. It was definitely more interesting than watching fair catches and just letting the ball be downed by the other team. The thrill intensified when I was on the actual field.

We only had a JV and a varsity team. My opportunities seldom came when I was a freshman and junior, but my sophomore and senior years were entirely different stories. I played both ways, meaning on defense, I was a defensive back, and on offense, I was a skill player. My speed allowed me to be a receiver, running back, or quarterback. I never wanted to come off the field, so I would go wherever the coach would put me. I preferred offense. For some strange reason, it never hurt when someone tried to hit me, but when I was on the other side of the ball and delivering the hit, it had the opposite effect. Even though it felt terrible, I am proud to say that I never backed down because my team needed me. In one game, I split my chin when tackling a ball carrier. There was blood all over my jersey, and the official made me leave the game. Since I did not want to be out of the game for very long, I made the paramedic run with me to the ambulance just past the end zone. She quickly put a bandage on my chin, and I returned to the game, missing only a few plays.

We played in an already-small school conference, but NBHS had the smallest enrollment of all of them. We were nonetheless optimistic my senior year; our confidence increased when we started conference play by defeating the Hampshire Whip-Purs. We were heavy underdogs because they had defeated perennial power Richmond-Burton the week before. It was rumored the Hampshire running back had over four hundred yards in total offense against them. Somehow, we were able to shut him down, and I was able to have a big game with 176 yards rushing. Despite this victory, we had a hard time competing the rest of the year because one of our best players went down with a knee injury. Harvard, Burlington-Central, Genoa-Kingston, and Richmond-Burton anticlimactically beat us badly. Like previous years, our record was not good enough to qualify for the playoffs. Luckily, in the basketball season, *every* team makes the playoffs.

If I had to rank the three sports, basketball would probably fall to the bottom. I loved competing, but my skill level was not great. I was an above-average defensive player because I was quicker than most kids. However, my shooting left something to be desired. Most times, if I was going to score, it was the result of a steal and a breakaway layup. My playing time was very similar to football: I saw a lot more of the court as a sophomore and as a senior.

Unfortunately, I missed most of my freshman season. After the first big deep freeze, I got the bright idea to go ice-skating on our pond. To make matters worse, I told my brother-in-law to throw me a football while I skated. His first pass was behind me, and I tried to lean back and catch it. I am not entirely sure what happened next, but as I fell awkwardly, I heard a cracking noise that had nothing to do with the ice. Charlie came over and helped me to my feet. I immediately knew my leg was broken. Charlie put my arm around his shoulder and escorted me up the hill to the house. I lay down on the couch with my leg propped up, waiting for someone who would take me to the hospital. My dad was taking his nap before work, but my mom decided to wake him with the news. As soon as he saw me, he said, "Stand up. I want to see you walk on it." I couldn't *believe* it. I wanted to say, "Are you crazy? My leg is clearly broken," but I also wanted to make it to my next birthday. I was the obedient son that I was raised to be. I slowly lowered my leg off the couch and put all the weight on my opposite leg in order to stand up. I gingerly tried to take a step and nearly fell over. As I hopped on my good leg, my dad conceded that we should "probably" go get it checked out. I was just relieved that he didn't just tell me to rub some Vaseline on it. That had been a family cure all for generations. In fact, members of my family rarely got stitches because my dad would just keep slathering Vaseline on the wound.

Our teams were mediocre, but that did not stop me from believing that if we worked hard, something special could happen. A remotely special thing occurred during my senior year. We lost to Winnebago in their Thanksgiving Tournament by thirty-six points. It was humiliating to be beaten that badly. As fate would have it, we faced them again in the Marengo Christmas tournament. I am not sure if I scored that game, but I was determined to not let the player I was defending make an impact on the score. We narrowly defeated them by two points. It was one of the most satisfying events of my high school career, and I was once the high scorer in a game with twenty points. That paled in comparison to this. Unfortunately, we were eliminated in the first round of the playoffs every year.

It was around this time that my brother Chuck returned home from Colorado. He had to move back in with us because he was very ill. The doctors initially diagnosed him with sugar diabetes, but he was not getting any better. He actually crashed his Dodge Rampage before they understood that it must be something more complicated. He spent a great deal of time lying on the couch moaning. I had never really spent any time with someone who was sick for an extended period of time, so I was convinced he was going to die. My parents are great people, but communication has never been their strongest suit. We just didn't talk about what was going on. I couldn't wait to get to school because I didn't like hearing or seeing him in pain. The parking lot would be empty when I got to school; I even beat the teachers there. I could hear the moaning in my head, and tears would well up. I tried to compose myself before entering the building, but many times I would just try to avoid eye contact until the redness disappeared. I didn't know what to say to my friends, so I just tried to pretend it wasn't happening. Sports were a great way to get my mind completely off it.

The spring was always my favorite time of year because it meant baseball season. A friend of mine wanted me to run track because of how fast I was. As soon as I found out that it conflicted with baseball, the answer was simple and definitive "No." He even suggested that maybe I could do both, but I knew that would not be fair to my teammates or myself.

I remember arguing with my sister about how bad her softball team was. She claimed that her team would be better if their coach had any clue. I said that they were not very good because her *team* was not very good. I discovered in my high school years that we were both right. I was disappointed when most of the coaches I had in high school were not up to the standard set by Coach Maitland. I am sure they did their best, but we were a ship without a rudder. I am not saying that the players had nothing to do with the outcomes of games, but it was clear to me that we were missing adult leadership. I understand how common it is for people to point the blame at someone else, and my parents raised me differently than that. However, there were several times when the things that happened during season embarrassed me, peaking especially when my coach was hitting "pregame" at Rockford Christian. He actually swung, missed, and fell down.

Regardless, baseball season always felt like home. I felt like a leader on varsity from the moment I was moved up as a sophomore. I even hit a double to the left center field gap for an RBI in my first plate appearance. I played nearly every position on the field. I am sure that was one of the reasons that I was promoted a level.

By no means was I without flaws. On one occasion in practice, I learned a valuable lesson about timing. I was playing third base when we simulated a fake pick play at second. Everyone was supposed to act like the pitcher threw the ball into center field. I spent a little too much time acting, and by the time I looked for the throw from the pitcher, it was literally one foot from my face. I could not get my glove up fast enough, and the ball struck me square in the nose. It did not hurt, but as I bent over, a faucet of blood poured out of my nose. I think some of the other players were freaked out as the pool of blood formed in the dirt. I just laughed at how stupid I was. I missed the end of practice because my nose was broken and my dad had to take me to the doctor, but I did not miss any more time. The next day, the pitcher apologized to me, and I assured him that it was entirely my fault. Part of being a good teammate is realizing when you make a mistake. I always worked hard at anything I did, but baseball seemed more natural. I finished that season being a solid contributor and couldn't wait for my junior year.

I wanted to help my team in any way possible, and that was no more apparent than in my willingness to pitch. It is a measure to how bad we were that I was one of our "better" pitchers. I enjoyed competing on the mound, but unfortunately, I did not baffle many hitters. I would guess we were about 0.500 when I took the ball. Luckily for me, I was a good-enough hitter that I got to hit for myself. There was a rule that you could run for the pitcher and catcher after two outs, but since I was so fast, I was always left on the base paths. At the end of the season, I was voted MVP and to the all-conference team. It was a nice honor, but I would have traded it in if we could have been successful in the postseason. That did not happen.

As I headed into my senior year, I talked to my coach about calling St. Francis on my behalf. There was no question in my mind that I would attend CSF, but I was hoping that they would be excited enough about me that I could get a baseball and, possibly, football scholarship. About halfway through the season, I was putting up relatively the same numbers as my junior year, and I asked my coach if he had made the phone call yet. I will never forget his response: "What do you want me to say?" I knew at that moment that he was not going to help me reach my dream. It was so *deflating*. I was crushed. How hard could it be to make a simple phone call and brag about one of your best players? For the first time, I doubted that I would end up at St. Francis.

My dad could tell something was wrong when I got home from the game. When he prodded me, I told him about my conversation with Coach on the bus ride home. He looked at me and, with a calming voice, said, "Don't worry about it. I will take care of it." He went over to the phone and immediately called Coach Shields, who was my football/basketball coach and the athletic director. He had only been at North Boone since the beginning of the year. He came to us from Providence St. Mel, where he won a state championship in basketball. Instead of complaining about the other coach, my dad simply asked if he would be willing to call Coach Gillespie on my behalf. Without hesitation, he told my father that it would be "his pleasure."

Just like that, my spirits were lifted. I believed that my dreams would get back on track. The next day, I stopped by Coach Shields's office to thank him. He told me that he had already talked to Coach Gillespie and that after what he told him about me, he decided to give me $4,000 to play both football and baseball. I stood there dumbfounded. How could everything turn on a dime so quickly? Then he looked me in the eye and said something that I could never forget. "Hey, kid, I staked my reputation on you, don't let me down." I knew that he was totally and completely serious and that I had to do everything in my power not to disappoint him.

Around this time, my family got some even better news. The doctors had finally diagnosed my brother Chuck correctly. He had a disease called hemochromatosis. Simply put, he had too much iron in his blood. His health would never fully return to where it once was, but he will continue to feel much better with the treatment. He felt well enough to tease me every chance he could about how stupid freshmen in college are.

A few weeks later, I worked out a much-anticipated return visit to Joliet. I remember being a little scared, but that all melted away when I walked into Coach Gordie's office. He shook my hand with a huge smile as he greeted my parents. We sat and talked for a little while, and in that short time, I knew I was where I was supposed to be. My instincts as a young man were spot-on: there is no one I would rather play for because of the way he made me feel. Two specific questions really created a special interaction.

After discussing various topics, He asked me about my batting average. As soon as I responded, he repeated my answer in a disbelieving voice and said to Coach Del, "Can you believe how lucky we are to get this kid?" This was more than likely a typical routine, but I fell for it hook, line, and sinker. Now I did not want to disappoint him either. I wanted to prove that I was the player that I said I was. My parents often told me, "When all is said and done, more is said than done." I did not want to be one of those people who talked a good game but could not back it up.

I also remember him asking what my favorite movie was. Without hesitation, I let him know that it was *Rocky*. Coach Gillespie then went on to name all the things about that movie he loved. He talked about the indomitable spirit of man, believing in yourself when no one else does, never giving up, giving it everything that you have, your heart is not something that can be measured, to name a few. I felt like we were kindred spirits when he said his favorite line was actually from *Rocky II*. He asked if I remembered when Apollo wanted a rematch and he asked his trainer Duke what he was afraid of: "I saw you beat that man like I've never seen no man get beat before and he kept coming after you." It was like we shared the same brain. Did Gordie know that I wanted to be Rocky because of everything he represented? I couldn't wait to show him my spirit.

I was oblivious to what a remarkable coach he was because he never used his accomplishments to "sell" the school. I focused on how he made me and everyone else around him feel. I was later educated on his incredible win/loss record and long list of awards. I learned that he was a successful coach in basketball, football, and baseball. He had even been inducted to several Hall of Fames in both football and baseball on the state and national level. He even played college basketball for the legendary Ray Meyer at DePaul. My dad admired the way Coach Meyer coached and knew without a doubt that Gordie picked up some valuable lessons from him. It was remarkable to me that he did not feel the need to brag about any of those incredible honors. I became even more enamored by his humility. It was no surprise to me that graduates would often stop in just to spend a little time with him. The more people knew Coach, the more time they wanted to spend with him. Players were shocked when they were in an airport with Coach Gillespie and a booming voice yelled out, "Hey, Gordie!" The man came over and gave Gordie a huge hug. As he pulled away, the players discovered that it was the one and only Ted Williams. Obviously, Gordie never felt the need to brag about the famous people with whom he was friends.

Near the end of my senior year, I drove to Joliet again. I wasn't able to see Coach Gillespie because his team was playing in the NAIA College World Series. The athletic office had just received word that the team had finished second. I knew that Coach had won three national championships at Lewis University but had been stopped shy of this goal at St. Francis. I now set my sights on a new goal: I wanted to be on a team that would bring Gordie his first national championship at the College of St. Francis.

My dad's field of dreams by our new house in the woods

Chuck and I at Phil's wedding. I wasn't always a headache to him.

Chapter 5

Freshman Year 1989–1990

T he ride to Joliet was under a two-hour trip, but it felt like an eternity when my parents drove me to drop me off because I was consumed by the thought that I was now responsible for myself. Growing up can be terrifying. However, I was amazed at how upbeat and happy everyone was as we unpacked the car. The family-type atmosphere calmed my nerves. My parents do not waste a lot of time with pleasantries, so when their mission was complete, they headed back home.

I was raised by people who didn't care a lot about periphery things, so therefore, neither did I. That became very obvious when I was left alone in my room with a TV and nothing decorating the walls. It almost felt like a prison cell. My roommate arrived a little later that day, and he didn't really have much to make the room feel any less bland. It was a bit of a culture shock when he told me more about himself. He lived on the outskirts of Chicago and went to an all-boys school called Brother Rice. My eyes almost popped out of my head when he told me that he and his buddies were chased by the police when they stole beer from a White Hen pantry. To make matters worse, he said that his dad was a Chicago police officer. We had football in common and not much else.

We arrived two weeks before the other students because that is when football practice started. Our first practice started at 9:00

a.m.; after several hours, we would break for lunch for a few hours and then resume for an afternoon session. It was nonstop football. I enjoyed playing, but at five foot ten and 170 pounds, I was a little undersized. I was shocked at how much bigger and stronger players were that I was facing. In addition, they were more intelligent and skilled than I was. I had a lot to learn.

I thought I was in great shape, but all the fundamental drills at running back and receiver taught me otherwise. Every day we would focus on key skills that we would need to perform in a game. I was taught to use precise cuts to hit holes provided by blockers or to create separation from defensive backs. The first three days, my legs were so sore that I had trouble walking. I was able to loosen them up again about ten minutes into practice. We eventually transitioned into learning and running the plays. The first time we ran a controlled intersquad game was the first time Coach Gillespie yelled *about* me.

I was playing a slot receiver and could not get off the line of scrimmage to run my pattern. The defensive back who was guarding me jammed me, and I couldn't get by him. After the second play with the same result, I heard Gordie yell out, "Somebody teach that farm boy how to get off the line!" I thought it was the most interesting way to yell at a player without directly yelling at them as an individual. Immediately, an upperclassman named Terry McCarthy taught me two four-letter words that solved the problem. They were called the *swim* and *spin*. The moves were so simple to learn because I just had to do what the word said. I could swim past the defender by pushing with my outside hand and making a swimming motion with my inside arm over the defensive back. The other move was just as easy. When the defensive back tried to jam me, I just spun away from the contact and continued my route.

Unfortunately, these moves were not applicable when I returned punts or did contact drills at running back. I had many collisions with players that had at least thirty pounds on me. I remember going back to the dorms with an awful headache. I would take naps between practices, but whenever I woke up, the room would be spinning for a little while. I thought it was just part of being a football player. My head would be throbbing as I put my helmet back on, but I did it anyway because I did not want to be considered soft by other players or the coaching staff. My brother Phil told me to get back on the horse, and that is what I intended to do. In my mind, I also thought it would be a form of giving up or quitting, and that was not an option for me. The public did not know anything about concussions in the late eighties. Looking back, it was clear that my attitude was dangerous to my health.

What worried me more was what I was missing at fall baseball. Coach Delgado was in charge since Coach Gillespie was busy with football. I was afraid that I was falling behind because the fall coaches could not compare me to the other players. There were only two other football players that also played baseball, and they were established upperclassmen. As my first college football experience came to a close, I started to wonder if I would be better off focusing on one sport. My passion was in baseball, and I doubted that I had enough talent to be more than mediocre at both. It is also a fact that I never left baseball practice with a pounding headache.

Most of my time at practice was spent with all the other running backs, regardless of their year in school. It was helpful to see how the upperclassmen performed drills and executed plays. Being around them enabled me to see what level of performance was expected. They also set the standard for being tough and ignoring the pain that was inflicted on a daily basis. During water breaks, the older running backs would ask me and the other freshmen to go out and drink with them at night. They were very surprised when I was the only one who declined their offer. My standard excuse was that I had just turned eighteen. They countered that with the idea of just hanging out at their apartment and getting loaded. I decided to just come right out and tell them that I did not drink. It really seemed like that was an unacceptable answer to them, and they really started to put on the pressure. It seemed as if they considered it a challenge to get me to drink with them. They started to treat me differently in practice because I said, "No." They would give me the cold shoulder and spend more time with the other running backs. It was very clear that I was "uncool" for refusing to get drunk with them. I was surprised that it really didn't bother me that much. My experiences on the farm must have made me confident enough to resist this peer pressure.

My parents always made their position clear on the subject. They would tell stories about people who would not show up to work on Monday because of what they were doing on their weekend. My dad considered it a waste of money because people would have nothing to show for it afterward besides a hangover. My parents also made me paranoid that it was somehow contagious. I saw that some members of my extended family were alcoholics, and I feared that it could be in my genetics. The biggest factor in my decision not to drink was the promise my dad made me. He asked me to make a choice between sports and alcohol and drugs. He told me, "You will not be allowed to play sports if I find out you are involved in the "other." I knew that I could take my father's word to the bank, so my decision was made. I loved sports and didn't want anything to keep me from playing them.

I think my dad was so opposed to it because he saw it ruin plenty of athletes. He knew that an athlete's potential would never be reached with alcohol or drugs holding them back. In high school, I was nearly the only person who didn't drink. My friends didn't mind because they knew I would be there to help prevent them from making bad decisions. My college football experience was not the same, but I felt secure in my decisions. I didn't care if other people drank; I just didn't want anything to hold me back from accomplishing my goals.

Our football practices were held off campus, so we had to get rides in both directions. At the end of one practice in late October, I realized that my ride left without me. As luck would have it, Coach Gillespie noticed and offered me a ride. I mustered up the courage to talk to him about my concerns in continuing both sports. I wanted to assure him that I was not a quitter and would honor my obligation if that was what it took to keep my scholarship. He completely understood where I was coming from and promised me that my scholarship would remain as long as I continued with baseball. I expressed my appreciation and guaranteed that I would complete the remainder of the football season and the full four years in baseball.

I was relieved that I was able to reach the end of the season without being seriously injured so I could focus all my energy on baseball.

At the conclusion of the season, all the freshmen football players turned in their equipment and decided to have a two-hand touch football game on the quad. I was on the opposite team of the all-state running back who came from Reavis High School. I always assumed that since he was all-state, he must be better than me. I was pleasantly surprised at the end of the football game that I had scored the majority of our touchdowns. During one play, I was in the open field and made a juke move so well on a stud defensive back that I went untouched into the end zone. My buddies ridiculed him the rest of the time. I covered the all-stater, and he only scored once. That experience taught me that I could compete with anyone and my speed was the key.

Before long, it was time for semester finals. I did not have difficulty allocating my time during the season, so it felt like I had an eternity to study for finals. The exams were not easy by any stretch of the imagination, but I managed to keep a solid B average. I was ready for a monthlong break. I caught a ride home from one of our basketball players who grew up near Rockford. He was willing to take me to the Clock Tower Inn, where my parents would pick me up. There was not a direct route there, so we took the back roads home. When we rode about ten miles on Caton Farm road, I got a big whiff of a hog farm. Without hesitating, I took in a deep breath and said, "Home." Chris almost had to pull over because he started laughing so hard. He was disgusted by the smell and couldn't wait to be past it. I, on the other hand, treasured it because I was raised that "it is the smell of money." He thought it was hilarious that home smelled like animal waste. My home did not smell that way, but the idea of what home meant to me was represented by that odor. The old adage was true: "You can take a boy out of the farm, but you can't take the farm out of the boy."

Months earlier, my parents decided to sell off the majority of our Black Angus herd. They wanted to take all their children, their spouses, and their grandchildren to Hawaii. I spent ten days in this paradise, and my biggest memory centered on a family football game.

We are a very competitive family, and I could not wait to demonstrate what I had learned at college. My brother Phil was probably as crazy as I am, so I decided to guard him. I started on defense and was able to prevent him from even running his pattern. I could tell he was frustrated and getting more and more furious. When it was my turn on offense, I knew he was going to try to jam me as retribution. He lunged at me as the ball was hiked, and my spin move caused him to lose his balance and land on all fours. I stuck up my hand to signify that I was open, caught the pass from the quarterback, and went the distance for a touchdown. I continued to frustrate him on defense and then baffled him when I used the swim move against him. Instead of torturing him the whole game, I decided to share how I acquired these new skills. We all agreed that failure could be a powerful teacher if you are willing to learn.

Christmas break flew by, and I was back in school before I knew it. I actually welcomed the second semester because that meant baseball was just around the corner. Most people love college because of the freedom of their schedule and the ability to sleep in. I organized my schedule so I could maximize my experience on the field. It was communicated to us that we would have early morning or afternoon practice inside until we could get outside. All games and outdoor practices would be in the afternoon. I set my schedule up accordingly.

Monday, Wednesday, and Friday, I would take classes from 8:00 am until 11:50 a.m. Tuesday and Thursday, I only had two classes, so I started at 8:00 a.m. and finished at 11:00 a.m. I made sure not to take any night classes in case games ran long. Many of my friends thought that my class schedule was brutal, but I did not care. I liked the freedom that my schedule gave me. It allowed me to focus and compartmentalize academics and athletics. I knew that to be a student athlete, I needed to take care of the student part first. I decided to attend every class that was within my power because there could be a spring trip for baseball, which would cause me to miss class. I wanted my professors to know I was serious about their class and give me the benefit of the doubt when I had to miss for my sport. My mother always taught me that half of life is showing up and the other half is working to the best of your abilities. Going to school even when I was sick was a lesson that stuck with me. Some players flat-out told me that they set their schedule so they could get a little break from baseball. I considered them fools because they would always have regrets for not giving their full effort. I knew in my heart that I had an advantage over them because my time on the farm helped me appreciate hard work.

When practices started, I saw some similar attitudes. At that time, I was on the JV team and playing the infield. Our fundamental drills were very intense and could be exhausting. The first chance we got for a water break, I took off my sweatpants because I was hot. One of the players criticized me and said that if I was smart, I could get another break by doing that during a drill. I knew right then that I would get more out of myself than he would. I always heard my dad talking about people wasting their potential. The thought occurred to me, how will I ever know what my potential is unless I work as hard as I can and then and only then will I have no regrets in my life. Little things like this could help get me closer to my goal.

Part of practice was spent in the racquetball courts hitting Wiffle balls. All the players would get one-on-one instruction when it was not their turn to hit. I was shocked to learn that Coach Boseo saw many flaws in my swing. He explained that every player here was a star on their high school team and, to compete, I would have to make some changes. He explained that the worst pitcher we will face would be better than the best pitcher we faced in high school. If we wanted the bat speed to keep up with them, adjustments needed to be made. I struggled to make changes but knew I would be more comfortable the more I worked at it.

I considered it a good omen when I received my first uniform. I was assigned number 18. That was the same number as my child-hood idol, Andy Van Slyke. Coach Maitland prepared us to wear our uniforms exactly like Coach Gillespie demanded. I knew I would discover other similarities the longer that I played for him. I did not play very often when the games rolled around. The coaches decided to move me to the outfield where I could utilize my speed. The opportunities were few, and I could see that other players were more talented. I was a little frustrated because I knew that some of them were selfish and not very good off the field. I had no control over that, so I just focused on my own efforts. Most days I was relegated to being a pinch runner and keeping a chart. I was determined to be a team player; my attitude would never be detrimental to the program.

We had a home game on a day where the weather started out very rainy. The field needed a lot of work if it was going to be playable. Most kids wanted nothing to do with maintaining the field, but the farm taught me to love physical activity. It felt like I raked in Diamond Dry / Turface for an hour. I remember overhearing Coach Lambert expressing his opinion to Coach Boseo that I should be in the lineup. He told him that we would not be having a game if it were not for me. His petitions did not make a difference; I was not in the lineup. However, it did teach me that people notice when you are selfless and will be in your corner. These lessons were preached by my family and Coach Maitland, and now I could see how they would help me at St. Francis.

I could tell by the end of the season that some players were going to transfer to another school because they did not agree with their position on the team. There were others who were going to hang it up because they recognized the warning signs that they would never be able to outperform the players in front of them. I maintained the positive outlook that if I continued to learn and work, I could reach my goals. I saw no reason why I could not become a starter if I continued to work hard and improve.

As the athletic and academic year ended, I was happy with where I was headed but not satisfied with where I was. I knew that the summer would be another opportunity to keep improving. My brother-in-law was able to get me a job that paid very well and had hours that fit into my summer league schedule. I worked for a company called Henkels & McCoy. We started early in the morning and were done with work by the late afternoon. Most of my games were played after 5:00 p.m. Honestly, I did not consider it hard work because most things that we did on the farm were much more strenuous. We pulled old cable out of the underground PVC pipe and replaced it with new fiber optic cable. The two hardest jobs were pulling off the manhole cover and cutting up the old cable that was about three inches thick.

My coworker actually got me a raise because I was strong enough to cut the cable and another worker could not. He wanted me to be paid as much as he did since I could do more of the work. Once again, I saw that hard work could pay off.

On the days that I didn't have games, I would run the hill by my house in the woods after work. I saw Walter Payton train on a hill, so why not try it? Even though I was a die-hard Packer fan, I could not help but admire the work ethic of Walter Payton. He exemplified physical and mental toughness by making it to the NFL from a small school in the south. It also reminded me of Rocky running up the mountain in Russia during *Rocky IV*. I would play the soundtrack on my little cassette deck as I trained. I did not have a place to work out, so I did push-ups and sit-ups every day. I would alternate days where I would run sprints or long distance. I wanted to be in top physical condition for fall baseball. Summer break was not much of a vacation, but I knew I would not fall behind other players.

Proof that I knew how to "hang loose" in Hawaii. I wish I had a picture of Phil eating my dust on the football field.

Chapter 6

Sophomore Year 1990–1991

During freshman year, I got my prerequisites out of the way but still had not given much thought to what I would do for the rest of my life. I was perfectly content to focus my energies on baseball and take care of business in the classroom so I would be allowed to do that. Fortunately, my college adviser kept planting the seed that I would need to decide soon on a major so I could graduate on time. There was part of me that wanted to get into sports medicine and be an athletic trainer. I figured that way, I could be around sports the rest of my life. Some advice that always stuck with me: "Find something that you are good at and love to do and it will never feel like you work a day in your life." However, I found out how much science I would have to take, so I eliminated that quickly. I actually visited Beloit College in high school with the intent of studying sports medicine.

There were not that many other options that fit my criteria. I enjoyed being around people, and I wanted to do something where I could make a real impact. Several of my siblings went into the teaching profession, and I enjoyed learning about history, so that seemed to be a natural path for me. I really did not do any type of soul-searching. It appeared to be the route that was most conducive to my plan. I decided to be a history major and eventually use that to become a high school history teacher. A large part of me just wanted to get the decision over with so I could set my schedule and engulf myself in baseball.

My favorite class was an elective class: team sport, baseball. Coach Gillespie taught the class. Most athletes took the class because they knew it would be an easy A to help their grade point average. This did not mean that it was a "blow off" class that athletes could skip and their coach would automatically give them a good grade. Gordie's integrity would not allow that. They also took it because of how entertaining it was. The class was always full even though it took place at 8:00 a.m. Gordie had more energy at sixty-four than all the twenty-year-olds in his class.

I was entertained from the moment he took attendance. After the first few classes, Gordie would call some people by a nickname; some of them made sense, but some of them were totally bizarre. For example, he would call his star baseball player, Alex Fernandez "Chico" or one of his offensive lineman "Big Polak." Multiculturalism had not yet reached Joliet. If someone arrived late to class, he might shout out, "You big walrus, you are just happy to find the building!" Some of his strangest nicknames were "Lemonade Stand," "Big Buffalo," "Tantor," and "Gypsy." From time to time, if someone was not paying attention, he would say "I am going to trade you for a dog and shoot the dog" or "Me Tantor, Me not know answer but me hit baseball far." No matter what Gordie said, it was impossible to think that he was being mean-spirited; he was just trying to liven up the class and have a little fun. Everyone could tell that he cared about them. Students were actually more upset if they were not called some nickname. I never saw him act in a malicious manner. Students paid attention in his class because they did not know what would happen next.

Sometimes he would teach a portion of the class using a Donald Duck voice. It was not uncommon for him to jog around the classroom, stand on his desk, or throw a ball to the student he was calling on. One day he was so animated in class that he had to excuse himself from the room. A few minutes later, his secretary came in to tell us that class was dismissed. We were afraid that we gave him a heart attack. He was right back at it a few days later. That is why, before I graduated, I wanted to take the only other class that he taught, psychology of sport. There was something about Gordie that made me want to be around him.

Fall baseball started right away because the season would end as soon as the cold weather hit. In northern Illinois, thirty-degree days can come as early as late September. Rarely did nice weather last until late October. We would be lucky to get in two months of baseball. The coaches would use this time to evaluate players. I was new to this process, so I did not know what to expect. We spent some time on the fundamentals, but we did not waste much time on dividing into teams. The coaching staff allowed the players to take ownership in this as long as the teams were divided evenly by talent, positions, and years in school. The coaches would also determine the pitching schedule.

Since I missed the previous fall, I initially felt out of place and to a degree like an unknown. The season became a blur. There were only a couple of things that stood out in my mind. I could easily identify the top players, and I was not one of them. Of course, there were some pitchers who had nasty stuff and threw the ball harder than I had previously experienced. However, I would marvel at the skill level of a few specific players.

A junior catcher carried himself with great confidence. Alex could do it all. He saw the field well and communicated what he saw with the position players. He gave the pitchers great confidence that they could throw any pitch at any time and he would block it. He was also able to eliminate base runners with snap throw pickoffs. He had the perfect combination of quickness with a strong arm. Pitchers could always tell when he was frustrated with them because he threw the ball back to them harder than it came in. He was also very accurate when runners tried to steal. He threw out nearly half the runners who tried to swipe a bag. He was on the varsity team since he was a freshman. He told me about his first at bat ever as a Saint. The team was behind in the game, and Gordie put the team in "plus one." That meant that the hitters needed to take a pitch until a strike was thrown. Alex came in to pinch-hit and was so excited to show Coach Gillespie what he could do that he forgot about the instructions. He hit the first pitch off the center field wall for a double. Gordie was furious and let him know it. Alex understood that even though he had a successful at bat, that was not part of the team strategy. In order for the team to be successful, everyone on the team had to follow the expectations without exception. If he popped out on the first pitch, the team would be in an even worse position. The strategy forces the pitcher to throw more pitches, which hopefully leads to more base runners. Coach only used this when the pitcher had control problems. Coach Gillespie emphasized the importance of the team over the individual. He believed that the only chance that we had to win a national championship would be if we were *all* pulling in the same direction. He knew that the most talented team wasn't always the team that won it all.

The player that I was most impressed with was our center fielder. Now that I had been transitioned to the outfield, I wanted to watch and learn from the best. Les was a five-tool player. He was fast, could hit for power and average; he was good defensively and had a great arm. Those five factors made him very appealing to scouts. When I arrived at fall ball one day, he was playing catch with Alex, but it was not normal catch. He was throwing the ball from deep center to the plate. The ball never got higher than head high the whole time, and it hit the target more times than not. I learned a lot about how to play the outfield by just watching him. Unfortunately, I also saw some things that should never be done. It seemed like he was not enjoying himself on a daily basis, especially when his performance was below his standard of excellence. Little did I know that his personal life was causing the majority of his stress. One day his emotions boiled over and he threw a bat so far that Coach Delgado banned him from fall baseball. It turned out to be a great lesson for everyone about what is and what is not acceptable behavior at CSF. I knew I would never reach his talent level, but I promised myself to never let my example in front of the team ever be a negative one. I wanted to make sure my actions were always positive and focused on the team. I really believed that just being positive could help bring us closer as a team.

It came as no surprise that Coach Gillespie was a guiding force during that difficult time in Les' life. Gordie had a knack for being a positive role model for his players. It never seemed to matter where or what we came from, he just knew how to help his players rise above their problems. That is exactly what Les did. We were all so proud when Les was able to overcome his own adversity and make it all the way to the Major Leagues with Kansas City. His faith enabled him to become a success on and off the field.

Philosophical and psychological lessons were not all that I learned that fall. I learned that I needed to keep working if I was going to have a chance to contribute to this team. I would need to work on my bat speed if I was going to hit at this level. I also needed to learn to simply not swing at pitches that I could not handle. The result of my at bats would be determined, as much by the pitches I did not swing at as the ones that I did. Swinging awkwardly at a breaking pitch or at a ball in a location that was difficult for me would just give the pitcher more information on how to retire me. Pitchers love it when batters get themselves out. That fall, they got me to pop out on high pitches, dribble grounders back to the pitcher on the inside pitches, and strike out on off-speed pitches in the dirt. I came to the realization that I should only swing at the fastball down the middle if I did not have two strikes on me. That is something that is easier said than done, but I saw plate discipline as an opportunity to get better.

The experience proved to me that I made the right decision to stop playing football. Even though I did not get to spend as much time around Coach Gillespie, there is no doubt that I would have fallen further behind in baseball since I was not a supremely gifted athlete. I was lucky enough to stay connected in some small way to football. I applied in the athletic office for being a worker at events. I became the spotter at football games. I thought it was a great job because all I had to do was watch the game and tell the announcer who carried the ball or made the tackle. I would help him with any other details that one person cannot see during the game. I would help calculate yards gained or lost, relay penalties called, and confirm down and distances.

Listening to the announcer planted a seed in my head that one day that might be something that I would enjoy doing. I would get to be around sports and people so it would be right up my alley. I learned several subtle things from this announcer. He did a great job of getting the home crowd excited without being too much of a "homer." He was also very accurate with his information. However, one night I was at a party with a bunch of football players. One of the defensive linemen was telling a person next to me that he was tired of the announcer giving the credit for a tackle to the middle linebacker. I jumped into the conversation with a laugh and said, "That must be my fault because I fed him the information." He backtracked immediately even though he dwarfed me in size and told me it was no big deal. I explained that it is very hard to see the numbers in the pile and if he could communicate to his teammates to turn and face the press box as they get up, we could identify them and be much more accurate. He appreciated that we wanted to get things right, and I appreciated him not squashing me.

During time-outs or between quarters, the announcer would play music or make announcements that he was required to do. A few years later, I remember a specific message that he delivered. Several times a game for several weeks, he repeated an advertisement for a new movie based on the life of a local citizen. The movie was called *Rudy*. This person actually played high school football for Coach Gillespie at Joliet Catholic High School. Little did I know that this movie would become a hit shortly after it was released because it appealed to the human spirit! The main message of the movie was about never giving up until you realize your dreams. I started to see this as a reoccurring message in my life. I was smart enough to see the similarities between Rocky and Rudy. They were both ordinary people that wanted to accomplish extraordinary things. They both inspired me to work harder and not give up when things get tough. If you want to accomplish your goals, you have to be resilient.

As football season came to a close, final exams rapidly approached. I found that I was prepared because I showed up to every class and was willing to work. I maintained a high B average in all my classes. I recognized a simple formula to success in the classroom: show up and work. I was never the smartest person in the room, but I was always in the room working. I witnessed a person on my floor fail out of school. He never showed up to class because he was playing video games. That seemed like a real waste of money to me. His mother must not have made him go to school with a fever as mine did.

My family did not go on vacation every winter break, so I returned to the farm until classes resumed. My family farm had a wooded area with plenty of old trees that had fallen over. I spent most of the break in the woods with my dad. He convinced me that chopping wood would be great for my swing and building up strength for more power. I really believe that my dad was not trying to trick me into working all break. He knew that this task would help both of us. He would use the chain saw to divide the trunk and branches into stumps. I would then take the splitting maul and split the stumps into manageable pieces to fit in the fireplace. Once again, I was reminded of a scene from *Rocky IV* where he was chopping wood to build strength for the upcoming fight. The trees helped a lot to block the cold breeze, but I would have welcomed it because I worked up a great sweat. It was actually fun spending time working with my dad, and it made break go by quickly.

It reminded me of a time when I was in grade school working in the woods with Pete and my dad. Dad was sawing the branches off the trunk of a tree that was lying on the ground. Pete told me to go up and clear away the branches to give Dad more room to work. As I approached, Dad turned around with the chain saw still engaged. Luckily, I was wearing four sweaters and it only ripped a hole in the first three. The holes were right in the middle of my chest. Dad's face went ghost white as he shut the chain saw off. Not a word was said, but I could tell how relieved he was that I was not hurt. I teased my brother that he was just trying to eliminate the favorite child.

The majority of classes that I signed up for second semester were within my history major. The same teacher taught a great deal of them. I had him as a freshman, and I could tell I would be able to handle any class that he taught. He was not a pushover, but he was an elderly man who obviously enjoyed what he did. I knew that if I showed interest in the material and asked insightful questions, he would help me get the grade I wanted. I was fortunate to build up a rapport with him and was glad to see him as an option every semester when it came to choosing classes. My academic life was lining up nicely.

I wanted to eliminate as many bills as possible for school, so I decided to apply for a resident assistant position. I actually applied in the middle of my freshman year, but the final spot was given to someone else. I could tell that they liked that I was not discouraged after being rejected the first time. I nailed the interview because I was more mature and had a good idea what they were going to ask me. I felt comfortable with the process, and I could tell that they felt the same way. A few days later, they confirmed my belief by giving me the job. I would not start until my junior year, but I was excited that if I did my job, I would have my room and board paid for the next two years. I knew the job would be easy for me because most of the residents were my friends and keeping things running smoothly should not be an issue. It did require some extra work, but it was dealing with people, and that is something that I enjoyed.

Before I knew it, the baseball team was preparing for the season and making plans for the "Southern trip." Northern schools always travel south at the beginning of the spring season so they can actually play games. The fields in the North are still covered in snow or frozen solid. Northern teams are stuck practicing inside at least a month longer than teams from the South. It is great to be able to see a real fly ball and how a ground ball bounces off the dirt instead of a wooden floor. At St. Francis, our options were limited to practicing in the gym or the Joliet armory. We were normally relegated to early morning practice because the basketball team was still competing. They would have the gym in the afternoon unless they had a game later in the evening. The coaches had a never-ending array of fundamental drills that we would perform in these facilities. Coach Gordie would preach the idea of muscle memory: if you train your body repeatedly when you get in a real game, your body will respond automatically. I now knew where Coach Maitland learned many of his drills.

The Southern trip took place for two weeks. It was always planned around a week that we had off school so we would only miss a week of classes. I was lucky enough to be selected to go on this trip as a sophomore. The coaching staff always took more players than they needed, so everyone could see what the expectations of the program were. I am sure I was the last person selected to go, but I wanted to make the most out of the opportunity.

The team would often travel to away contests in large passenger vans, but for a trip of this distance, the college hired drivers and a Greyhound bus. The upperclassmen always chose the back of the bus, so by the time I got on the bus, the only seats available were in the front with the coaches. I did not mind this because I knew I was bound to learn something new by just being near them.

Some players would sleep, while others would play euchre for the entire trip. I had never heard of the game before but was able to pick up how to play by watching and asking questions. Euchre was a four-person card game where you worked with a partner to get at least three "tricks" with trump cards. The first team to ten was the winner. Several groups would play, and if you got a partner, you were welcome to challenge the winning group. Of course, there were also many stories being told about previous trips and shenanigans that players would pull when coaches were not around. Other players would talk and tell jokes or just move around the bus and visit with different teammates. The bus had a bathroom, so we only stopped for gas. The trip flew by even though it was about eighteen hours long. I would spend some time just gazing out the window looking at the fields. I loved seeing how the farmland was different in other states. In Texas, I saw a farmer bailing hay into round bales. I told the coaches that those were illegal in Illinois. When they asked why, I responded, "Because cows can't get a square meal." They just laughed and shook their heads. My dad's sense of humor struck again.

I will never forget the first hotel we stayed in as a team. Shortly after we were settled, I heard a bunch of laughter coming from the hallway. At least half of the team was crammed into the entryway of a player's room we all called Tooki. He was probably the strongest guy on the team, and he was built like it. His frame was probably what enabled him to entertain us so easily. Many of his "shows" required him to be only partially dressed, and this was one of those times. He had poured some water on the tile of the bathroom floor. He had taken his shirt off and was lying on his back in the middle of the puddle. He would proceed to do an abdominal crunch; when he made this move, the water would be squished between his back muscles and make a loud noise that sounded like flatulence. Everyone there would roar with laughter and run to get other teammates to witness the spectacle. The best part would be how Tooki would giggle every time he heard the noise as if he was in third grade. We never got sick of his performances because they made the trip so memorable.

My dad was able to retire from the Chrysler plant in Belvidere my freshman year of college. My father did not have to work the farm because of a program developed by the federal government. The program paid my dad not to plant crops in order to keep the supply lower and farm prices higher. Both my parents decided to get out of the cold and head South for the winter. They purchased a motor home so they could go to a different Southern destination every year. Since I was traveling with the team, they decided to follow us around. Three years earlier, they followed my sister's college team around in Louisiana. My mom was actually fired from her job at the end of this trip. My parents wanted to catch a few more games before heading back. My mom called back to her job, and they would not allow her to extend her vacation, but they said she could call in sick. She knew that would be dishonest, so she refused that option. Most people would think she was crazy, but that was typical behavior for my family. She believed that her true character is more important than anything else is. What a great example of integrity for me to try to live up to. Her example showed me firsthand that the truth is always the best policy even though it is a rare trait.

The schedule was full of games against great teams. In two weeks, we squeezed in as many as eighteen games. It was not uncommon to play a doubleheader, especially if we happened to be rained out. Most of the teams we played were in the NAIA. In previous years, we heard stories of our Saints' team taking on and defeating a loaded Mississippi State team with the likes of Bobby Thigpen, Will Clark, and Rafael Palmeiro. Performing like this against that caliber of teams caused NCAA teams to rethink playing our small NAIA school. Coaches realized that even if they were able to beat us, their ranking could go down. Coach Gillespie always wanted us to see the best competition, because if you want to be the best, you have to face the best, and by the end of the year, we would not be intimidated by anyone. The regular season was all about preparing for the conference and the postseason. The other players admired the plan that Coach put in place for us. He knew we would take a few on the chin along the way, but in the end, we would be better for it.

An additional difficulty in playing these teams was that they had been practicing and playing outside since day one. Our first time outdoors was when we stepped off the bus. Gordie never let us make excuses. He believed that we were prepared and should be able to execute the fundamentals of the game in order to be successful. He knew that these experiences would strengthen our resolve as individuals and as a team. Whether we won or lost, Gordie would always have a short postgame meeting going over the positives and negatives of the game so we would know how to improve. His focus was always on getting better each game. We could tell that the coaching staff hated to lose, but we would be treated the same regardless of the outcome of the game.

After games, we were issued our meal money; luckily, it was regardless of our performance on the field. Many times, we would go to a restaurant as a team, but if we had a taste for something else, we were allowed to branch out with other teammates. Early on in the first week of the trip, I ended up eating with Coach Gillespie, our star center fielder, and several other players. We laughed and joked about a lot of things, but the conversation always returned to baseball. Somehow, the topic turned to who the fastest player on the team was. Most players assumed that Les was the king of speed, but I was shocked when he looked at Coach and said that I could outrun him. Gordie looked at me with disbelief, but I just shook my head in an affirmative manner.

That was all Gordie needed to hear. The next day, I was the courtesy runner for the catcher. This rule was established to speed up the game by allowing the catcher to get his gear on while someone else ran for him. Most players would not be thrilled by this, but I embraced it. I figured it could be a way I could get on the field and contribute on a daily basis. Deep down, I was also hoping that if I performed extremely well, then just maybe my role would be expanded.

The next morning, a few of us were walking to breakfast before our game. It was a dark and cloudy day, and Todd Sipple said, "It looks like the game might get rained out." I looked at the sky and inhaled deeply before I said, "It doesn't smell like rain." He just laughed and shook his head at me. After breakfast, we paid our bill and walked out of the restaurant to a downpour. Todd took one look at me and said, "Does it smell like rain *now*, farm boy?" I guess not all lessons that I learned on the farm were accurate.

That trip provided two very vivid lessons, and the first one was about failure. We were playing at Texas Wesleyan, and I came into run for the catcher. I had to dive back into the bag repeatedly because the pitcher was anticipating that I would steal. As soon as he started his motion to home, I took off, I felt that my jump was not great, so I slammed on the breaks and returned to first. The catcher threw a perfect strike to second, which surprised me a little because he was a lefty. That is highly unusual at the college level. You would think that I would figure that there must be a reason that he is catching, but I remained undaunted. The next pitch, I got a great jump on the delivery and tried to swipe the bag. It was a bang-bang play, but the precise throw nabbed me. For a moment, I thought I must be safe because of the way Gordie reacted. He was yelling to the bench, "Have you ever seen a better piece of base running?" "That was awesome, that is how we do it." He did not need to say anything more. We all understood that we should stay aggressive and failure is part of the game. If you do everything correctly and the opponent executes perfectly, you just have to tip your cap and try again next time. Gordie was always teaching.

A situation while playing Sam Houston State University provided a completely different lesson. We had a talented sophomore who both played a position and pitched regularly. In fact, Ivan Lawler played on the varsity as a freshman. On this particular day, he singled in a run and advanced to second on the throw home. Later in the inning, he was thrown out at third, and instead of sliding, he went in standing up. What transpired next actually scared me as a player. The color of a Gordie's face, coupled with his snarl, was enough to relay his message. Just to be sure that he was clear, he immediately replaced him in the lineup and said something to the effect of "If you ever want to play in this program again, you better give your full effort." Hustle was expected of every player at all times. Lack of playing time can also be a great teacher.

It was clear how much Coach cared about us. We knew that when he was hard on us, it was for our own good. It was like having another father. I will never forget a game we played at Texas Northwoods. It was unforgettable for two main reasons. One, there was a beautiful rock formation just beyond the fence in center field. Two, I stole second base, but I got a bloody nose as I dove into second. Gordie walked out, reached into his pocket, and took out his clean white handkerchief. I didn't want to stain it with blood, but he reached out and held it to my nose. It didn't take long for it to stop, but he told me to keep it in my pocket in case it started again. I washed the handkerchief after the game and tried to return it to him the next day. He told me, "Hold on to it, you never know when you'll need one." This was an example of how he cared more about people than he cared about objects. I kept that handkerchief in my pocket for every game I ever played for him. I even carried it in my pocket when I became a coach after my playing career was over. It reminded me to care more about my players and share anything that I had with them.

Near the end of the trip, a unique situation occurred that created a new learning experience for the whole team. We were in the late innings of the second game of a doubleheader. It seems like ballplayers get bored after a long day on the diamond and need to find ways to entertain themselves. Gordie was old-school and wanted players to always be in tune with what was going on in the game. That did not deter people from being a little mischievous when Coach was entrenched in the game.

One of the pitchers decided to pull an old prank on a fellow pitcher. Each of these pitchers had been recently used and had no chance of pitching again that day. Kevin attached a few matches to a six-inch piece of tape. Mike was distracted considerably because he was having an in depth conversation with our pitching coach, Joe Heinsen. Kevin actually crawled under the bench while his team-mates' legs provided cover. With stealth-like precision, he lightly attached the incendiary device to Mike's sock. He lit the fuse and sneaked away. Before we knew it, Mike was jumping up and down while swatting at his leg trying to figure out what was going on. The "hotfoot" was executed so perfectly that a small hole was burned in the sock, but no real damage was done to his flesh. The confusion in the dugout was greeted with a growl of disappointment from Coach Gillespie. He made himself clear that he would deal with us at the conclusion of the game.

The postgame meeting had an entirely different tone than what we were accustomed. Gordie's disgust for our behavior was written all over his face. He made his expectations perfectly clear, and anyone who did not wish to meet them could excuse himself from the pro-gram. He always told us that if we were not part of the solution, then we were part of the problem. The team then lined up on the foul line and ran sprints until Gordie thought it was enough. He asked the majority of the team to pick up our equipment and get on the bus until Kevin was finished. We sat on the bus for what seemed to be at least thirty minutes as Kevin continued to run sprints. By the end, his "sprint" had slowed down considerably. The punishment was not over as we watched Kevin take deep breaths with his hands on his knees before his next set. What we saw next really surprised all of us. Gordie was "running" the last few with Kevin. He was in his sixties, so the speed was not there, but the message was, no matter what mis-takes are made, they will be dealt with quickly and fairly, but it is for your own good, and in the end, he will be there for you. He will not hold a grudge when it is time to move on to what is next. I think all of us appreciated the gesture that Gordie made to Kevin. It helped us realize that we must stick together as a team no matter what. He solidified his bond with his players by simple acts like this. We were still a little terrified of him, and the bus was completely silent on the way to our next destination.

It was very rare that we returned to Illinois with a winning record, but that would not prevent the coaching staff from emphasizing how competitive we were, and to them, that would equal success. We battled every game, and by the end of the year, we would be on the same level as those Southern teams. On our way home, we stopped to play Greenville. They were located several hours south of Joliet. We won the games easily, but what stood out to me was the individual performance of our catcher, Alex Fernandez. Early in the game, he picked a base runner off second base. A few innings later, he picked a runner off first base. I knew the team would not try to steal on him after they witnessed that, but I also anticipated that they would shorten their leads off the bags. I was wrong. Late in the game, Alex completed the trifecta by picking a man off third by basically jumping over the batter and making a perfect throw. It was a feat that I had never seen before and probably never would again.

I split time between JV and varsity the next several weeks. When I got an opportunity, I did not make much of a case for myself offensively. Even though I struggled at the plate, I returned to varsity as the runner for the catcher. It was clear that this was the extent of my role. I cannot say that I was extraordinary, but I was effective and not a liability on the base paths. I spent a lot of time with other bench players, and I noticed yet another way that Coach Gillespie communicated and conveyed lessons to players. If a mistake were made in the field, instead of directing his attention there, he would address the dugout. He would explain what should have been done and then asked if we understood. He knew that bench players could be thrust into the lineup through necessity, injury, and graduation. He wanted to make sure everyone was prepared and would not make the same mistakes. His common sense approach continued to impress me.

One of Gordie's most memorable teaching moments occurred at the beginning of May when we made a road trip to SIU Edwardsville. During one of the games, our first basemen did not catch a pop-up in foul territory that appeared to be an easy out. With a snarl on his face, Gordie turned to the dugout and said, "What are we, a bunch of spastics out here?" As he turned around, a backup infielder looked at us and started to fake convulsions as if he were a "spastic." I didn't know what that meant, but Todd's acting conveyed a clear picture. It caught me by surprise, and I nearly laughed aloud. Miraculously, I was able to stop myself. I am sure we would have suffered his wrath if we were not taking the game seriously. We knew that Coach always wanted our heads in the game.

These "nonstarters" knew the game and anxiously awaited their opportunity. As playoffs approached, I remember them discussing who would make the playoff roster and who would be left off. I had no idea that the number of players finishing the year in uniform would be any different. On one road trip, an upperclassman explained to me that at this point, I was more valuable to the team than he was since he was a third-string first baseman. It turned out that we were both on the roster but not everyone could say the same.

The first round of playoffs was a blur, and before I knew it, we advanced to the next round where the stakes were higher and things became more complicated. We were in Anderson, Indiana, and we became the only undefeated team in a double-elimination tournament. Some of the guys started to tell me about Lewiston, Idaho. This was the usual site of the NAIA World Series. They explained that there were several thousand people at every game. Some fans would be asking all players for autographs before and after games. They all loved the ballpark, which was home to Lewis-Clark State College. There were even stories about how assistant coach Tony Delgado took players on hikes to see waterfalls on off days. Apparently, on an off day when Coach Gillespie was scouting, he took the rest of the staff sightseeing in the mountains. They were nearly killed on a narrow road when a logging truck came around a tight corner.

Coach Del played shortstop for Coach Gillespie at Lewis University. He must have been a tremendous athlete because he was also the point guard on the basketball team. He loved adventure and apparently invited any interested players to tag along on his hikes. He admitted later that Coach Gillespie might not have been thrilled to find out some of the dangerous positions some star players put themselves in on these treks. These players described Idaho almost as a magical place. Everything sounded so spectacular that I knew I wanted that experience even more. The goal was well within our grasp.

The next games happened to be on the same day as graduation at St. Francis. I was shocked to learn that a few of the senior players were going back to be a part of the ceremony. It seemed odd to me because I viewed it as a piece of paper that could not compare to this once-in-a-lifetime opportunity. They had already met the requirements for graduation. In my eyes, the ceremony was not imperative. I could only speculate why each individual would make that decision. I knew one of them had already pitched previously and could not come back to the mound again that quickly, but I felt like if I were in his shoes, I would want to be with my teammates to celebrate. Regardless, they decided not to stay. I don't know if that had any effect on what transpired next.

The next game was in fast-forward for me. Before I knew it, we had a 2–1 lead and only needed five outs to advance the World Series. If you could image a nightmare inning, the eighth was just that. It was like watching an accident in slow motion, knowing there was nothing you could do to stop it. Without reliving every painful second, let's just say that two runs scored without the ball leaving the infield. A 2–1 advantage was now a 3–2 deficit. In the world of baseball, that is not a big deal, but as I looked around, I knew in my gut that I would not be visiting Idaho this year. Even though we had our turn at bat and another game if necessary, I knew it was over. Most of the players had given up, a characteristic uncommon to Saints teams led by Gordie. My biggest regret was not saying something when I recognized the problem. I thought to myself, *Who am I? I am only a sophomore runner for the catcher.* By not being part of the solution, I felt partly to blame as we succumbed 5–0 in the second game and watched the other team celebrate. It was devastating to be so close and watch my dream slip away. I promised myself that I would learn from that experience and never remain silent in a desperate time again.

The season was over, and there was nothing to do except let that feeling fester inside. Whoever said "I hate losing more than I love winning" was spot-on. Not knowing if we would ever get that close again tormented me, but all I could do about it was get back to work.

Chapter 7

Junior Year 1991–1992

The fall semester started a little earlier in August for me since I had RA training. We actually went to a facility called Iron Oaks to build unity among the resident assistants. There was a lot of team building and leadership activities to help prepare us for the arrival of students. After lunch, we prepared to tackle the "ropes" course. We each had to put on helmets and harnesses for safety since we would be working together to climb obstacles. Since it was a summer day, I was wearing yellow athletic shorts that I got when I played football. When I put on the harness, it conformed to my body, making it appear as if I were wearing an athletic supporter. Immediately, one of my buddies said, "Hey, Paul, did you steal a sandwich from lunch?" We found out that laughter can be great for team building as well. I am glad my parents taught me not to take life too seriously, because everyone had a joke about me for the rest of the day.

I was assigned to Marian Hall, which was a dorm for mostly freshmen and sophomores. The main part of my job was to make sure that the residence hall was a home away from home. I helped students feel comfortable by answering any questions that arose and made sure things were fixed in a timely manner. Making sure students were respectful to one another and school property at all times was probably the biggest challenge. Definitely, a balance needs to be learned about having a good time and not disturbing other students who are serious about their academic career. Problems were rare and minor. I once had a freshman ask me if his girlfriend was going to break up with him. I laughed and said, "Probably, most couples do when they get to college." I learned that being direct with some people was not always the best approach.

This job allowed me to focus on academics and athletics. Nothing remarkable was going on in either area. I continued to go to class and put in enough effort to remain an A/B student. Fall ball started as soon as school resumed, and we were there every afternoon unless it was rained out. I was working hard but cannot say that I was taking strides forward. In fact, I could see that if I would continue to perform this way, there would be no way I would earn a starting position in the spring. Little did I know that the situation was worse than I anticipated.

About halfway through the fall season, Coach Delgado pulled me aside. He looked me straight in the eye and said, "Paul, the coaching staff has determined that you will never play at St. Francis. You are a tremendous young man who works really hard, but you will never see the field. You are more than welcome to be part of the team as a courtesy runner, but that is the only time you will play." I remember just taking it all in calmly and nodding my head that I understood. To be perfectly honest, quitting never even crossed my mind. I was disappointed and wanted more than anything to prove them wrong, but I wasn't sure how to do that. At first, I thought, *Maybe I should just work every day on my speed and become the best base runner that they have ever seen.* Then I reconsidered and decided to do what I was always taught: show up and work without complaining about my situation. I planned on doing everything I could to intensify my efforts to improve at every facet of the game; I knew I would never give up on myself and the possibility of playing. I believed that I could change his mind if I improved enough. Regardless of what my future held, I was determined to be a great teammate.

I motivated myself by repeating over and over in my mind, *You'll never play.* Every repetition I took was more dedicated than the one before. I refused to let anyone know about the situation. I would let it fuel me without changing my attitude. I hoped that people around me would see my resolve to improve my skills. Everything I did that was baseball related had to be with a clear purpose. There would be no way to change their minds if I did not become somewhat obsessed with this goal. I knew that even if I fell short, I would be proud of who I became because I didn't give up on my dream. I still had over a year to become what they needed.

Anytime I played catch or threw from the outfield, it was with a renewed purpose. My speed allowed me to have great range in the outfield, but now I wanted to increase that. I also knew that my speed was worthless offensively if I could not get on base. I knew I needed to double my efforts in hitting. I did not go out with friends much because I wanted to spend down time working toward my goal. I reserved the racquetball court so I could hit Wiffle balls regularly. One time, I asked my friend Ed Soldan to pitch to me. It was a good thing that we were great friends because we wouldn't have survived this experience if we weren't. I was so frustrated with him because he could not throw me a strike from only thirty feet away. I didn't want to create bad habits by swinging at bad pitches, so I hardly got to swing at all. It was a wasted hour of our time. I learned my lesson to never ask a tennis player to do anything baseball related. In spite of this experience, I believed that my hard work was bound to pay off, whether it be as a junior or senior.

The fall and winter came and went, and I treated each day as an opportunity to improve in some way. I was unable to hit and throw every day, so I worked on getting stronger. I did push-ups and sit-ups in my room as if I were in a penitentiary. I would have a workout partner in my room when I cued up a *Rocky* movie to the training montage. I would rotate watching each of the movies because it felt like I was experiencing some of the same scenarios as the main character. I liked to think of it as a quest or healthy obsession. Building myself would be a gradual process of a daily commitment. I really felt that I was growing as much mentally through this process. I knew that I would have no regrets if I gave it everything that I had.

As spring practice rolled around, I continued to keep my nose to the grindstone. I maintained a positive attitude and used practice as a method to improve my skill set. I could see the lack of intensity in some of my teammates, and I believed it would only be a matter of time before I passed them in ability. My dad consistently preached to me the rewards of hard work and hustle. "Hustle beats talent when talent doesn't hustle." I am not sure who first said that, but it sounded right out of Dad's playbook. At no point was I rooting against the other outfielders, but I began to see that my desire would be the great equalizer.

The Southern trip was a similar experience to the year before, but with a few additions. On this trip, we brought along one of Gordie's friends who was a tremendous baseball fan. We all called him John "Da Barber" because that was his profession and he would cut any player's hair for a discounted rate. I can testify that he was about the only barber in the area who could cut a good flattop. Even though Drago (Rocky's opponent in *Rocky IV*) had this haircut, I wore my hair in this style to pay homage to my dad, who wore it like that for nearly forty years.

John sat in the front with the coaches. We thought he actually dressed like a coach because he wore an all-white sweat suit with a Texas Longhorn on it. It must have been a sign because we stopped to get gas somewhere just shy of the Texas border in Oklahoma. We all got out to stretch our legs and get snacks. The bus was parked next to all the semis as we returned with our corn nuts and candy bars. Quite a few of the players and Da Barber had stopped to check out all the steers on a cattle truck. As I approached, everyone started to scatter and then burst out laughing. One of the steers relieved himself through the vents in the side of the compartment. The excrement sprayed all over John and his white warm-up. It definitely wasn't the whole load, but it was enough to leave some big brown spots. I think John was more furious at us for laughing so hard at him. Needless to say, he headed back into the restroom to remove as much as he could. There was no doubt in my mind that this story would become legendary on future trips.

We arrived in Arlington, Texas, and stayed there for several days. Our hotel was right next to where the Texas Rangers played. Unfortunately, we had some rainy weather that canceled a game while we were there. Most of us anticipated that it would be a day off. We learned that there were no days off with Coach Gillespie. We used the parking lot to get in at least an hour-long practice. Coach had planned ahead and packed "Kemko" balls. These are rubber baseballs that are the same size and weight of a real baseball. These would enable us to do all the drills that we would normally do without ruining baseballs by getting them waterlogged. Coach knew that this would prevent players from hoping for rainouts. When players saw bad weather coming, their focus switched to game mode because that would be way more fun than practice, and that was exactly what Coach wanted.

After practice and dinner, a small group of us decided to wander over to the ballpark and see what we could see. We were shocked when we discovered that the main entrance was not very secure. The fence was only ten feet high and was not designed with any barbed wire or spikes at the top. That was basically an invitation since it was clear that they couldn't be completely serious about keeping people out. Most of us scaled the fence and climbed down the other side. A few were actually skinny enough to squeeze between the gate since the chain had some slack to it. Once inside we had free reign of the seats and field, unfortunately the doors to the clubhouse, concessions, and offices were all locked. Believe me, we checked them all. It seemed too good to be true. We wandered the whole stadium checking out the view from different seats. When it became clear that security was absent, we decided to visit the dugouts and field. Just sitting on the bench could cause anyone to dream about making it to this level of the game. We ran around the bases and the outfield.

As it got dark, I had someone stand on the mound and throw me a golf ball that I found. It was dark enough that I could not see it fly to the outfield, but I was able to hear it land in the seats. About that same time, we realized that we were not alone. A couple of security guards came up on either side of us. We could have tried to run, but we knew someone would be caught and we didn't feel like we were doing anything wrong. I guess we had never heard of breaking and entering. They sat us down in the box seats and asked us what we were doing. We were completely honest and told them we were from Illinois playing baseball. They immediately asked,

"Would you sneak into one of the Chicago MLB stadiums and play around?" We responded in unison, "If we could get in!" They didn't find it humorous, but we weren't trying to be funny. One of the security guards whispered something to the other and disappeared for about ten minutes. I started to worry that he was going off to call the police. I shared this idea with our senior captain, Alex Fernandez. He looked at me and said with a smirk, "Don't worry, nothing is going to happen."

My mind was racing a million miles a minute about what could happen to us. Would we need to be bailed out of jail? Would the coaches send us home? Would we be kicked off the team? I had always been a rule follower. Up to this point, I had never even gotten a detention in school. The only thing that calmed me down is that we did not damage anything. We were just in a place we should not be. The second person returned and did his best "bad cop" impersonation. His general message was about how lucky we were that he did not call the police and that if he catches us in there again, that is exactly what will happen. He walked us to the gate, unchained the fence, and let us go. As we walked away, I saw him take the slack out of the chain so no one could fit between the gate.

A day later, a few players ignored our story and climbed the fence at the ballpark again. It was pitch-black in the middle of the night, and a few of them, who will remain nameless, decided to run the bases naked. The first player joked that he never ran so fast because he was afraid the other player might catch him. Luckily, security never even knew that they were there.

I was relieved that the coaches and my parents would never find out. My parents were again following the team no matter where we went. I would have had to tell them what happened if the security guards turned us over to the police. Many of my teammates grew close to my parents since they were always around. They cheered for every player and knew each of them by name. Many players would talk to my parents even before I was able to after the game. The team admired their dedication to me and the team.

The results of our games were typical. We were playing teams who have been at it awhile, and we were still shaking the rust off.

Our record would indicate that we were not as successful as we would like to be. However, as the Saints' media guide demonstrated, it was part of "Gordie's Youth Movement." The cover photo showed Gordie in the dugout with nine of his grandchildren wearing St. Francis jerseys. In reality, the coaching staff had recruited a bunch of young players and many of them were going to play as freshmen. I really didn't think it would have an impact on me because most of them seemed to be infielders. I didn't take into consideration that some older infielders might switch to the outfield to avoid losing playing time. Naturally, there is a learning curve from high school to college baseball, but these youngsters adjusted quickly.

Even though Gordie was in his midsixties, he still brought a youthful exuberance to the ballpark every day. He would show it in little ways by commenting on the weather like "It is a great day to play a great game, laddie bucks." Sometimes he would jump into our pregame hitting stations. He would take over pitching Wiffle balls and tell the hitter that there was no way he would be able to hit him. He would act surprised if the player was able to make solid contact against him. He would go as far to say, "No one in the history of the game has hit me so hard." I was afraid that he would keel over after he threw for twenty minutes one hot Texas day. Gordie would just take a break and tell another player, "See if you can get him out." This was his way of getting us to give our best in monotonous drills. If the old guy was going to nearly give himself a heart attack, the least we could do is give our best effort. He believed that those efforts would pay off once the game started.

Our freshmen shortstop learned a valuable lesson from our senior catcher. After striking out, this newcomer to the St. Francis way turned and threw his bat toward the dugout. Since I was only running for the catcher, I would also make sure the bats were in the dugout at the end of the inning. Alex stopped me from going to get the bat and called his teammate over for a "chat." Without embarrassing him, he informed him that he will pick up his own bat and that behavior will never occur again. To both their credit, I never saw that again from him or anyone else on the team. That was another example of how Gordie's expectations and respect for the game were so clear that he did not have to correct players himself all the time; his players would take care of it for him.

Despite the fact that we were playing as many as four freshmen in the first two weeks, we had compiled a winning record at 11-10-1. The opponents from the Sooner state ranged from Oklahoma Baptist to East Central State to Oklahoma City. The Lone Star state provided teams like Mary Hardin–Baylor, Texas–Arlington, Dallas Baptist, Sam Houston State, and Texas Wesleyan. It was a possibility that we could see any number of these teams in the World Series at the end of the year. Since we were holding our own at the beginning of the year, I believed there was no reason we shouldn't be able to outplay them at the end of the year. I felt like the trip was an encouraging sign for getting to that elusive national championship. First, we needed to continue to improve and compete for our conference title.

On April 1, we were scheduled to play our crosstown nonconference rival, Lewis University. Their mascot was the Flyers, and they had a small airport on the campus. I called my parents and told them that the game had been canceled because a student was killed when they crashed a plane in center field. I informed them that the wreckage had been cleaned up but the game was canceled out of respect for the student who died. About twenty minutes later, I called them and asked if they were coming to the game. They were very confused because of our previous conversation. It was about my tenth year in a row of pulling the most outrageous April fool's prank ever. My favorite one was when my mom slapped me in church because I fooled her that someone had assassinated Jesse Jackson. They asked if the joke was on me when we lost 4–3.

We played a few nonconference games at home before heading out on another road trip to a tournament hosted by Bellevue, Nebraska. This was actually a split squad game. Half of the team stayed back and played Illinois Institute of Technology while the rest of us headed out for a night game against Mayville State in Nebraska. The trip there was terrifying because in Iowa, we drove through an absolute downpour. I drew the short straw and was the one driving. It was raining so hard that I could barely see the car in front of me. That car belonged to Gordie, and if I lost him, I wouldn't know how to get there because it was still before everyone had cell phones. I felt like I tailgated him during the whole storm. To make matters worse, he was driving about seventy miles per hour. Luckily, the heavy stuff only lasted about twenty minutes. We were also fortunate that the storm did not hit our destination.

We arrived with just enough time to loosen up and play the game. We only had eleven players. The only two on the bench were the relief pitcher and myself. I had several responsibilities that night. I was the courtesy runner, scorekeeper, bull pen catcher, played catch with the left fielder between innings, and called out "runner" if the opponent was trying to steal. Unfortunately, I was the emergency person if someone got hurt. Strangely, it never occurred to me that other people in my position might be a pouting jerk. I wanted to do whatever I could to help the team. I wish it could have been on the field, but I was not, so why waste my energy focused on things that were out of my control? I think my teammates saw how genuine I was, and I would like to think it inspired them to care more about the team than themselves. I heard a few of them laugh when I told Gordie to take one of my jobs when I went to the bull pen to warm up the next pitcher. I didn't want Gordie to think I was not committed to each of my jobs.

We won 9–1 and got word that we also won 8–4 versus IIT. Our full team would be together for our afternoon game the following day against Hawaii Pacific. I only remember this because each room received a pineapple as a gift from this team. Alex Fernandez was so excited when he saw this and couldn't wait to cut it up. No one in our room seemed interested except him. He went searching for a device to cut into it. I was sure that even though I had never tried pineapple, I would not like it. I could not have been more wrong. Alex just laughed when he saw my face after the first sample. It was like eating candy that was nutritious. I couldn't believe how much I loved it. Alex just kept repeating, "I told you." As soon as we devoured our tasty treat, I went to visit other rooms to see if they did not want their pineapple. One other room was foolish enough to relinquish what I now considered a prized possession.

I felt a little guilty that we didn't have a gift for them, and to add to that, we defeated them 5–2. That night, I was still obsessing over this delicious fruit until we were just hanging out flipping through channels. We stopped on a movie that none of us had seen, *House Party*. We laughed so loud that a few players came by to see what was so funny. They went back to their rooms to watch it as well. The movie became the topic of conversation on our van ride back to Joliet.

In the month of March, we were just over the 0.500 mark. That tournament helped catapult us to a 26–8 record in April, and at one point, we won nine ball games in a row. Unfortunately, of the six losses, three of them were to conference foe Olivet Nazarene. That put us in second place behind our rival to the south. However, none of that really mattered since the playoffs started at the beginning of May. The host of the district playoffs was none other than the team we wanted revenge on, Olivet Nazarene. The three losses to the Tigers in the regular season did not dampen our enthusiasm at all. Only one of the contests was lopsided at 3–10. The other losses were by a total of three runs. The double elimination format of the playoffs would benefit whoever was playing the best at the present moment.

We knew we could beat them, and in the first game of the play-offs, we got our opportunity. They were averaging almost six runs a game against us, and we were scoring less than three against them. Fortunately, our pitcher threw a gem and held them to only three runs. Our offense put up seven runs in a decisive victory. Our next game was against another conference rival, the Cougars of St. Xavier. During the regular season, we shut them out in two games but lost 9–4 in the other matchup. We were excited after our first playoff win, but Gordie would never allow us to be overconfident. I don't know exactly what or why it happened, but we lost 9–1. That meant that we were one game away from elimination.

Olivet managed to win their next game and force yet another rematch. The game was well played and close the entire game. The Tigers took a three-run lead in the later innings. In each of those innings, we put runners on but could not get them in. We were able to put runners on again in the ninth inning, but even though we were in the heart of the lineup, we were down to our final out. Our senior DH, Tooki, was up to the plate representing the tying run. He hit a ball to the hole at shortstop, which he was able to backhand and make a long throw to first. There was a collective gasp from the dugout as Tooki dove into first base. The umpire raised his right arm to signal that he was out and our season was over. That valiant effort made me realize instantly that I was now heading into my senior year and only had one opportunity left to bring a national championship to St. Francis.

His desperate dive into first signified how quickly a career can end and how players will do anything to try to extend it. I knew that I had at least 365 days left to avoid the same demise. The sands of my baseball hourglass were trickling down, and now I could see them rushing away more clearly. The only possible way I knew to extend my time playing the game I loved was through hard work. Only time would tell if I worked hard enough.

On Deck For '92

COLLEGE OF ST. FRANCIS

1992
Baseball
Media Guide $2.00

The cover of the 1992 CSF media guide

Coach Gordie Gillespie works on proper batting techniques with Paul Babcock of Poplar Grove.

Chapter 8

Senior Year 1992–1993

S ummertime meant one thing to me: one last chance to relentlessly pursue my dream of winning Gordie a national championship. I knew that in order to be successful, I would have to have a healthy obsession with my quest. I must be dedicated in thought as well as in my deeds. I made a plan to be in peak physical condition by training every day of the year. I had heard that Hershel Walker did five hundred push-ups and sit-ups on a daily basis. I saw no reason why I could not put in the same amount of time. Every day I would make time to run. As in previous years, I would alternate between long distance and sprint days. The *Rocky* soundtrack would again accompany my workouts. Many of the songs referred to the word "heart." I was hoping the coaches would see how big my heart was in my senior year.

I knew I must also prepare myself mentally. During my work-outs, I would still continuously repeat, "You'll never play." It was not done maliciously. I wanted to push myself harder and prove to myself that I could play. I knew that I had some impact as a courtesy runner, but I did not feel like it was enough to influence the outcome of a game. I felt I would need to be on the field contributing more often if I was to have any control over us going all the way to the title.

Before I blinked, it was time to return to school for RA training. The football team was back in the dorms and move-in day for the rest of the student body was upon us. My position was in Tower Hall, which was reserved for juniors and seniors. I was excited about this because most of the people on my wing were my friends that would not cause any real problems. Residents launching water balloons or bottle rockets out of windows were not of great concern to me. That would allow me to focus on the only thing that really mattered to me: training for baseball.

My course schedule was set, and I knew exactly what I needed to do to graduate on time. I planned on student teaching the fall semester after I graduated because tuition would be cheaper. I was hoping to be a graduate assistant coach the following spring if I did not get a job in the middle of the year. All that sounded too grown-up for me. I was in no rush to become an actual adult. The whole concept terrified me. I was glad to have an idea of what my future held, but I decided to live in the present moment each day, and the rest would take care of itself.

Before the fall season began, I got up the courage to go talk with Coach Delgado. This was Coach Del's thirteenth year as Gordie's assistant coach. We all knew how much Coach Gillespie loved him and trusted him. Their relationship went all the way back to when Del played for Coach at Lewis University. Del was even inducted into their Athletic Hall of Fame. I knocked on his door, shook his hand, exchanged a few pleasantries, and got on with the business at hand. I simply looked him in the eye and said, "Don't forget about me." I could tell he knew I would do anything I could to help this team. I am not exactly sure what he said to me, but it was something to the effect of "Keep working, Paw Paw, I'm rooting for you."

I could tell at the first day fall ball that my chances of playing had increased for the simple fact that a few outfielders had transferred. I was relieved that they made that decision because I knew in my heart that they were not "team" players. I could tell they were more talented than I was, but they were selfish and didn't have the heart and determination I believed were necessary to be successful. I had read enough about the Packer teams under Coach Lombardi to see that Gordie was trying to build the same type of atmosphere. He wanted his players to care more about the success of the team than their own success. That key ingredient could separate us from other teams. I did not see those qualities in the players who left. Coach Gillespie sold me on the idea that we all owed it to one another! Coaches owe players the preparation and hard work just as the players owe that to one another and the coaching staff. We were dependent on one another if were going to be special. He knew that few teams ever realize this.

Even though those players were gone, I knew there was no guarantee that I would play. I had to give the maximum effort every day to be considered for the starting lineup. It was clear that my arm strength had improved and that I had become a solid defensive outfielder. Although my hitting was not spectacular, it was obvious that I had improved. Each day my confidence grew to the point that I believed I had a real shot at being penciled in as a left fielder, but my opinion didn't matter. I hoped that I did enough in the fall to impress Coach Delgado, and maybe I would be in his conversations with Coach Gillespie.

As soon as the weather turned, I found two great lifting partners. Dan Samuilis was another senior who played both outfield and first base. He played more than I did the previous year, but his future playing time was uncertain and he had something to prove as well. One of the reasons he was playing the outfield was because of our final lifting partner. As a junior in high school, Dave DeHaan was an all-state first baseman for the Andrew T-Bolts. As a freshman, he was platooning with Samuilis at first. Both of them had a lot of power, and I am sure Gordie was looking for a way to get them on the field at the same time. Dan actually asked if he could work in the outfield so he could be more versatile for the team.

We decided to lift weights every day except Sundays. They were the best partners because they were reliable. We knew we could count on each other to show up every day and work. We had a great rapport and encouraged each other every step of the way. I know we rotated days between biceps and back, chest and triceps, and shoulders. We spent two days a week on each muscle group. We would also run and work on an abdominal routine. I remember the exercises that were absolutely brutal. We would perform three sets of ten pull-ups/chin-ups with three different hand positions for a total of ninety. That exercise was not as exhausting as our bicep routine. We would complete ten repetitions of the heaviest weight and then grab the next bar that was only five pounds lighter. We would repeat this until there were no bars left. It would look hilarious when we would struggle to finish the last set at a very lightweight. We were in great physical condition by the time the season rolled around. Looking back, the only area we did not focus on was developing our leg strength with squats.

One day, Coach Gillespie called a meeting on the balcony for all male athletes regardless of the sport that they played. We had no idea what it was about, but we knew it could not be good. We were able to decipher through his speech that it was about the behavior in the dorms. Gordie's face was bright red, and he was shaking his head and accidentally spitting as he talked. He was so angry that it sounded like he said, "Fishies in the microwave?" Apparently, someone decided to put human feces on a plate in the microwave in one of the lounges. College kids can act like animals, but Gordie was not going to sit by and allow this behavior to continue. At one point in his speech, he said, "Where are the seniors? Where are the leaders? Where are the captains?" I thought that all those words described me, and I hoped Gordie realized that I knew nothing about the situation. His respect was very important to me and the other players. I never found out who did this, but it never happened again.

My dorm room also became a laboratory of sorts. I knew that I would also need to be mentally sharp if I was going to help the team. I know many people thought I was out of my mind when they would hear *Rocky* continually coming from my room. I loved to watch the movies on my VCR and listen to the music on my tape deck. Logically, I knew he was just a character created by Sylvester Stallone, but in my heart, he was just like me. It was a story about the indomitable spirit of man. It was about being told you weren't good enough and proving to yourself that you can do anything that you put your mind to. It was not uncommon for me to act like a prisoner in a cell with nothing to do but push-ups and sit-ups. I would replay my favorite scenes over and over again in my head. The message was always the same: "Never ever give up."

There were only three other seniors besides myself on the 1993 baseball team. I only realized this because two of them were selected as captains by the coaching staff. Paul Chovanec was a relief pitcher on varsity his previous two seasons and convinced the coaches to convert him to a starter. He knew that Coach Gillespie did not use relief pitchers a lot once the season was in full swing. Ivan Lawler was both an outfielder and starting pitcher who had been contributing significantly to the varsity as an underclassman. I think most people would agree that he was the best player on our team. Both Dan Samuilis and I were disappointed that we were the only seniors, not captains. I decided to take the attitude that I did not need a title in order to act like a leader. Fortunately, for both of us a short time later, we were named captains as well. I teased Chovy that he just didn't want one of the responsibilities that came with the job.

Captains were required to get up even earlier for 5:30 a.m. practice because we had to drive the vans. We would have to pick up the keys at the security desk, scrape the ice off the windows, and get the engine warmed up. We had a ten-minute drive to the Joliet Armory, so one van would wait outside each dorm until about 5:10 a.m. We had "Gordie time" just like the Packers had "Lombardi time." That meant we needed to be ten minutes early if we wanted to be on time. When all was said and done, it took about an extra half an hour to do this job. Almost everyone would prefer the extra thirty minutes of sleep, but captains did not get that luxury. Luckily, we made it to practice safely every day even though one time I was so tired that I ran a red light. Fortunately, at that time of morning, no one else was on the road, but I woke up in a hurry when all the back seat drivers were screaming "Red light!"

The Joliet Armory had a large indoor space for us to practice. They had a gym floor that used to be a basketball court and two batting cages on either side. Coach Gillespie brought plenty of energy to every practice regardless of the time slot. Players were equally impressed by the level of intensity that Coach Tony Delgado brought. He was a dynamo. Players had to go hard in drills because of how hard he made them. Sweat would be pouring off Coach Del because of how quickly he would move. He wanted to make sure players got as many repetitions as possible in a short amount of time. Players often commented, "He could run a practice in a phone booth." His players gave a great effort because they would feel guilty if Coach worked harder at practice than they did.

Coach Joe Heinsen was our pitching coach and was the oldest member of the staff. He was like a wise old sage to the pitching staff. He was so old that he brought his own fold-up stool so he could sit as he coached. His main method of instruction was simply talking to players about little changes in their mechanics. The only demonstrations that he would perform would be to show how to grip the baseball for different pitches. Players could tell how much information he had accumulated during his life in baseball. Occasionally, he would share lessons that he learned from Major League pitchers with whom he worked.

When the 1993 spring sports media came out, the cover photo was of Gordie in a black jacket and cowboy hat. Inserted in the top left corner, it said, "32 wins away." Right in front of Gordie's face was a poster of former USC baseball coach Rod Dedeaux, and the caption read, "Wanted Dedeaux's Record." Gordie himself would never mention that if we won 32 games that year, he would become the winningest coach in college baseball history. Coach Dedeaux had 1,332 victories, which was more than any other coach in America. Coach would always downplay the significance of the record. He would say things like "It is a record of longevity" or "Wait until you see all the losses." I am not completely sure why it was not a priority for him, but I am sure the main reason was that he cared more about his players and their productivity in society after college than the success they had in college. He had also been so successful before this that it was probably just one more inevitability in his career. He was the head football coach at Joliet Catholic High School when they won several state championships. One of those players went on and had a successful NFL career with the Chicago Bears. He coached people who later played in MLB. He also won three national championships when he coached baseball at Lewis University. Gordie himself played basketball for the legendary Ray Meyer at DePaul University. It is quite possible that he always knew the day would come, and he saw no reason why his players should spend any time focusing on it. He always wanted us to focus on giving our best effort in every game so we would not have any regrets. It was always about us and never about him. That is one of the many reasons I admired him so much. He was so special because he was so humble and selfless. We wanted to get him the attention that he deserved. We knew that since he coached at this small school in the Midwest, most people outside baseball had never heard of him. As a group, I knew we would do everything within our power to get him to that milestone quickly.

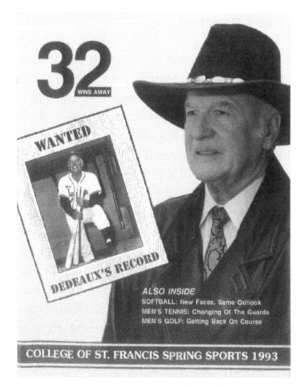

The 1993 CSF media guide cover photo

We started our quest on March 2 in Texas versus TCU. We were facing none other than Reid Ryan, son of pitching great Nolan Ryan. One of my first goals came true; I was starting in left field because Ivan Lawler was our starting pitcher. I knew that the only way I would remain in the lineup was if I played well enough to stay there. I only remember one at bat against him because of the impact that it had on me. I grounded into an inning ending double play. I was frustrated because I never thought a "speed guy" should be doubled up. In the process of trying to prevent this, I felt a twinge in my hamstring as I ran through first base. I was afraid that if I left the game, I might never get another opportunity to start, so I grabbed my glove and headed out to left. As I ran out to my position, I realized how selfish I was being. I would not be able to forgive myself if I could not make a play that could cost my team the game. That feeling trumped the urge to prove how tough I was, and I signaled to Coach Gillespie that I was injured and could not continue. It now occurred to me that we should have been working on the muscle groups in our legs as well. Until I healed, I would only be able to help my team by cheering on their efforts. Unfortunately, we lost the game to the Horned Frogs 9–0, and Ryan had eight strikeouts.

The next day, we dropped a doubleheader to University of Texas, Arlington, with a combined score of 14–4. We played Northwood (Texas) before turning around and playing Dallas Baptist. Both of these games resulted in losses that averaged a differential of five runs, 17–7 to be exact. The captains decided to call a team meeting and jam all our teammates in one of our hotel rooms. The highlights consisted of simply telling the guys not to panic and we are a better team than our 0–5 record indicated. Our message was clear: we will win consistently when we eliminate our mistakes. It was important to stress continued hard work and determination. We wanted to make sure players would not give up on themselves or the team. We also explained that the first several weeks are a grind that will ultimately prepare us for the end of the season. It was definitely an honest conversation about persistence when tough obstacles arrive. There was no guarantee that things would turn around immediately, with the stiff competition that we were continually facing. We knew this gauntlet would test our character and we should embrace the opportunities it would present to make us better in the end. Even though the four captains delivered the message, it was clear that we had learned these lessons from Coach Gillespie the previous three years. We were simply the vehicle to deliver the motivation.

Since I was unable to play, I wanted to make sure I was a leader in the dugout. I believed that talking with players and being positive each day was a way to contribute. I was doing my best to aid the healing process with physical therapy. It was actually good that I did not continue to play because the injury would have been much worse than a simple strain. I was hoping to return in a little more than a week. After our little powwow, we did not lose! We tied Tarleton State 3–3. Immediately after the game, we faced Oklahoma Baptist and defeated them 6–3. The next day, we again played two different teams. We beat Bellevue (Nebraska) 5–1 before again ending in a tie against Incarnate Word (Texas). The next two days saw four straight losses to Tarleton State and Southeast Oklahoma State, which brought our record to 2-9-2.

The games against Southeast Oklahoma seemed to drag on forever. It was a hot day without a cloud in the sky, and that spelled trouble for the catcher in the bullpen. There was no shade whatsoever for him to get out of the sun. About halfway through the second game, someone noticed that Matt's face was bright red. Gordie heard us talking about it, and he made his way down to the bullpen. He took one look at him and knew he needed to do something. What he did next entertained all of us. Gordie reached into his pocket and pulled out a Chapstick. He examined it and found where it said SPF 15. He unscrewed the bottom so the stick extended out about a quarter inch. He put his left hand behind Matt's head, and with the other, he started to apply Chapstick all over his face. When Coach was satisfied with his work, he returned to the dugout. Coach demanded that, between every inning, his bench players run down to the fence and back to ensure that our legs were loose in case we needed to go into the game. As the pack of us ran past the bullpen, we could see several chunks of Chapstick on Matt's face. We all burst out laughing at how ridiculous he looked. Gordie meant well, but I doubt his "sunblock" helped much. These little times of laughter did help us get through our early struggles.

After the game, we showered in their locker room before driving to Montgomery, Alabama. We didn't have a game scheduled the day we arrived, but we were scheduled to play five games in the next three days before heading home. We managed our third win of the year against Auburn–Montgomery. The following day, we dropped two more games, and I was able to play. Unfortunately, I was disappointed that I did not help the team offensively and even made a mistake in the outfield. Gordie called me up to the front of the bus to ask me how I was doing. I told him that I was concerned that I was hurting the team at the leadoff spot because I was not producing. He turned the conversation around by saying, "Remember that ball you hit hard but right at the second basemen, then the ball you hit just foul down the left field line?" "I bet you would be a lot more confident if those are hits." "This game is about confidence. Stick with it and believe in yourself, and things will be just fine." Gordie was a master of psychology. His pep talk definitely changed my attitude.

The final day of our trip, we were slated to play Auburn–Montgomery, followed by Oklahoma City on the same field. In the first game, I was in the lineup but now in the nine hole. In my second at bat, I checked my swing on a curveball, and I felt something "pop" in my bottom hand. My hand was throbbing when I tried to take a practice swing. The next pitch was low and on the outside corner for a called strike three to end the inning. I grabbed my glove and ran out to the outfield. I was flexing my hand as I ran out to my position, and I could tell something was wrong. It even hurt to squeeze my glove shut, but I could do it. There was no way I would take myself out of the game again if I could perform fully. Over the final two innings, only one ball came my way, and it was a routine base hit that I returned to the infield. I feared that I would not be able to swing the bat if I had another plate appearance. I decided that if it were a critical situation, I would inform Coach Gillespie that he needed to pinch-hit for me. Otherwise, I would use my speed and bunt for a base hit. The latter situation arose, and unfortunately, my bunt was not good enough to get me on base. We lost the game, and I was relieved that I was not in the lineup for the next game.

I could feel my hand swelling up during the game. I hoped keeping my batting glove on would prevent further swelling and keep anyone from noticing. We lost the game 8–1, which brought our record to a dismal 3-13-2 mark. One of the worst spring trips St. Francis has ever had. Offensively, our team batting average was 0.212. Defensively, we committed thirty-nine errors, and our pitchers had an ERA of 5.23. At this rate, it did not look possible to get back to 0.500, let alone get Coach to his next twenty-nine wins. Coach Gillespie, who was the eternal optimist, confided in his coaching staff, "Let's face it, we are not very good." This was something his team would never hear.

That night at dinner, my hand had swollen to twice the size. As I was leaving the restaurant, I spotted Coach and decided to show him my injury. He took one look and said, "I am so sorry, Paul." That reaction confirmed my belief that it must be a serious injury. The bus was supposed to leave the next morning for Illinois. However, Mother Nature had other plans. That night, it snowed a little over one inch, and we were stuck in our hotel for three days. All the highways were closed down because vehicles were in ditches all over the place. Southerners do not have snowplows, and they certainly do not know how to drive in icy conditions. It was a good thing that we got along as teammates because we spent a lot of time together in one another's hotel rooms.

I took for granted all the time we spent together because I did not realize that not all our teammates were that fortunate. Kerry Paprockus especially loved the spring trip because of all the comradery it provided. As a senior at Montini Catholic High School, he narrowed his choices down to CSF and Lewis University in Romeoville. Both of those were close enough for him to save money on "room and board" by commuting from Bolingbrook every day. He chose St. Francis for two main reasons: he would get a chance to play for Gordie, and his brother was a senior there. Most days after practice, Kerry was headed home when we were going to hang out. All the time that we spent together really helped build a special bond. Kerry was in catch-up mode on the spring trip.

When we were finally able to return to Illinois, it was confirmed by our trainer that I had torn ligaments in my left hand. He said that it would be a minimum of six weeks before I could swing a bat again. I still wanted to help the team in any way that I could so he made me a half cast that could keep my wrist and hand immobilized during games. I was back to running for the catcher, but it was better than missing the majority of my senior season. I had done that job for the last two years, so I knew I could help the team in that capacity. In practice, I made sure to get in some one-armed swings every day. If I was able to come back at the end of the year, I didn't want to be completely rusty. When I was growing up, I saw a movie called *A Winner Never Quits*. I decided to watch it because the title resonated with me. The movie was about Pete Gray, a player who made it all the way to the major leagues with the St. Louis Browns in spite of the fact that he lost an arm at six years old. If he could overcome this huge obstacle, I could survive this temporary setback.

Going home to Illinois had a profound effect on our game. Maybe there is something to sleeping in your own bed and eating in a place that makes you most comfortable. We did not play at home every day, but being back in the North made a world of difference. We won our first four games and averaged seven runs during that span. We split the next four games, but each of our losses were only by one run. Immediately there was a different feeling in the air. It was like we all woke up and said, "If somebody can beat us, so be it, but we won't keep beating ourselves."

Winning six of eight ball games was great kick start to the most fantastic winning streak that I have ever been a part of, and yet we did not even pay attention to it. We just went out every day and tried to play to the best of our ability. We did not count how many we had won in a row. We simply tried to show up and win *that* game, nothing more and nothing less. We were taking care of the business in front of us. We were entering conference play on a hot streak. Three losses put us in second place last year, so there was little margin for error.

Paul Chovanec took baseball seriously, but he also realized that we needed to have a little fun along the way. During a game when we had a substantial lead, he dared a freshman pitcher, Steve Ochman, to try some chewing tobacco. He convinced Steve that he would not get into the game and everything would be fine. Paul was wrong on both accounts. A little later, Ochman was asked to get loose and ended up going into the game even though he felt a little dizzy. The first hitter of the ninth bunted, and Steve threw the ball fifteen feet over our first baseman's head. Paul just shook his and giggled to himself. Steve had the last laugh as he struck out the next three batters.

We rattled off seven straight conference wins and twenty-two in a row over all. During that run, we could tell that we were generating a buzz because more students were coming out to the games. Even though I was not quite medically released, a bunch of my friends would come to the games and cheer us on. Between innings, they knew that they could get my attention when the "bench guys" ran down to the fence between innings. This was also the exact same time that the press box played music. My buddies decided it would be hilarious to change around a few words of a popular Bonnie Tyler song that was played every game. The song was called "Holding Out for a Hero." Their new lyrics were "He's gotta be strong, he's gotta be fast, and he's gotta be *named Paul Babcock*." They would yell the final three words as loud as they could, and I could not help but laugh. The atmosphere around the ballpark was becoming very special.

The weather was perfect for a ball game in mid-April, but my spirits were dampened during our pregame stretching routine. Paul Chovanec was stretching next to me when, out of the blue, he looked at me and said, "You're not hurt, you could play." My eyes welled up with tears as I replied, "You don't think I would give anything to be able to play?" Chovy loved to tease people, but this time, it backfired because I thought he was serious. He put his arm around me, kissed the top of my head, and said, "I'm sorry, Paul, I was just joking around." I am sure I was just a little oversensitive and slightly depressed that I was not healthy yet. I felt even closer to him after that because of the real empathy that he showed me. It reminded me of how we became friends in the first place. I always wanted to surround myself with quality people because my parents convinced me that it was contagious. Paul and I went to mass together one Sunday during sophomore year. He whispered to me, "Let's go right after communion." I was raised to stay the whole mass, so I did not respond. After communion, I was pleasantly surprised when he returned to the pew. After mass, he said, "I thought more about it and realized that I am not so busy that I need to leave early." That little event showed me that he was a man of integrity.

My teammates became very close to my parents because they had missed very few, if any, games over the last three years. Since it was my senior year, they coerced other family members to come with them. I was not surprised when someone new showed up. If they were babysitting my nieces and nephews, they had to come along because they would not miss a game. Most days they would stick around to congratulate the guys on what they did that day and then take me out to dinner.

My mom was sitting on the top row of the bleachers down the third baseline at one of our home games when a high foul ball hit her right between the eyes. She must have been watching the grand-kids because she did not even see it coming. She didn't even react when it hit her; she just slowly lifted her right hand to her face like she was thinking. Everyone in the dugout told me that she was hit, and I agreed, but her reaction made me think that I just was seeing something. She hated to draw attention to herself and did not want anyone to worry about her. Our trainer went over and confirmed that she was struck right on the bridge of the nose. He made her use some ice even though she didn't want any more attention drawn to her. Two days later, she looked like a raccoon because of her two black eyes. She just laughed it off. She was a great example of how tough farmers are.

Near the end of April, my parents asked my resident director, Christie, if parents were invited to graduation; she gave them the information. When she ran into me later, she couldn't believe that I did not let my parents know about this "important" day. I simply told her, "I know I will graduate, but I have no idea how long this season will last. I need to make sure it will last as long possible. I can't afford those distractions." Of course, she thought I was a little crazy, but I learned a valuable lesson my sophomore year and would not forget it.

The next two contests were a little more important to our team than any others were. On April 28, we traveled four hours south of Joliet to take on McKendree College in a doubleheader. The outcome of the games were never in doubt because this was the day that we could solidify our coach as the winningest coach in college baseball history. In game one, we jumped out to an early lead and cruised to a 20–1 victory. The record-breaking game was also decisive at 13–3. It was clear that Gordie wanted to shake hands and move on. He was never one to want to be showered with attention. I had no idea at the time, that by the time Gordie retired from coaching only one other man would have more total victories. That coach was Cornelius Alexander McGillicuddy, better known as legendary Connie Mack who coached the Philadelphia Athletics for fifty years. We were more excited than he was, but that did not stop his fans from planning a special celebration.

We did not arrive back on campus until about midnight. That did not prevent the students from enthusiastically greeting us in the parking lot. As soon as we pulled in, there was a roar of a large crowd. They were clapping and cheering for a man that had influenced their lives on campus. He knew that they were celebrating him as a person more than his accomplishments on the field. There were plenty of athletes from other sports waiting to shake his hand. Students who didn't even play sports joined them. They were there because Gordie cared about people and they wanted to show that they cared for him in return. His smile that night will be forever etched in my mind. In an interview that night, he said, "The victories would mean nothing to me if I didn't have the respect of the students." The students showed him how much they respected him.

Two days later, another milestone was reached with a victory over conference foe Illinois Institute of Technology. This was Coach Gillespie's seven hundredth win at St. Francis. The memory of our horrific start was erased by our new expectations of playing great baseball on a daily basis. May 1 rolled around, and there were only three games left before playoffs started. We took a short trip over to

Rensselaer, Indiana. The Pumas of St. Joseph's were our twenty-sixth victim in a row. This surpassed the mark set by a team at Lewis University that Gordie led all the way to the national championship in 1975. That information would not be shared with us until the season was over, however.

The winning streak was similar to most in the fact that different players were chipping in every day. Some impressive individual performances were delivered along the way as well. Early in our conference schedule, we played against the Cougars of St. Xavier University. Our left-handed first baseman hit a ball over the right field wall that struck the dormitory about halfway up the building, and it was at least fifty feet beyond the fence. Sometimes students would watch from their rooms and heckle us as the games progressed. Dave DeHaan made them think twice about that with one mighty swing. Paul Chovanec had quietly pitched his way to a 9–0 record. His next start came against the team that eliminated us the previous season, Olivet Nazarene. Chovy shut them out as we won 3–0 and clinched the conference title with only one game to play against the Cougars.

The final conference game was at home, and in typical Coach Gillespie fashion, he used this opportunity to "tune up" before play-offs. He had a knack for being able to prioritize what was really important. He knew that having all players ready for a playoff run was more important than how many games that we won in a row. Make no mistake about it, he wanted to win the game, but that had never been what he emphasized. It was more important to be prepared for any scenario that may arise in the postseason. The game was actually during finals, so our star player, Ivan Lawler, did not make it to the game until the fourth inning.

The game was tight the whole game, and we had a great opportunity to come from behind and win if it had not been for a miraculous line-dive double play made by the third basemen in the ninth. We had the bases loaded and the heart of the order coming up. Instead of having the winning run on second base, the game was over along with the streak at twenty-seven in a row.

I would not be surprised if Coach secretly welcomed the loss knowing that it would be one less thing to distract us or create a little extra pressure that players imagine this time of year. Losing now was a great reminder of how badly losing stinks. We hated losing more than we enjoyed winning. We knew the formula for winning was great pitching, defense, and timely hitting. It was time to put that knowledge to work when it meant the most, in the playoffs.

At the conclusion of every regular season, the coaches hosted a banquet for the players and parents. The coaches took the opportunity to deliver a clear message about the next step, recognize the accomplishments of the season, and give out some awards. The message was the same every year, but it was always sincere. "We are the team to beat." The coaches always believed it, and this year, I believed that all the players did as well, but believing it is different from proving it.

The night started with parents, players, and coaches reminiscing about the highlights of the season. I was prepared when the awards ceremony rolled along. Obviously, I knew I would not be mentioned for any great athletic accomplishment, but there was another award that meant more to me. It was called the Joe Heinsen Award. It was named after our pitching coach who had been in baseball for nearly fifty years. In fact, he was the bullpen catcher for the White Sox and Cubs the last time they appeared in the World Series. The award was given to the player who exemplified spirit and teamwork. I was honored with the award as a junior and was hoping to be the first player to win the award twice.

Coach Delgado got to the podium to say a few words about what the sportsmanship award meant to the school. He talked about the qualities that coaches look for in student athletes and how often so many of the qualities are elusive. Many athletes have some, but it is very rare when a student has them all. He then read this portion that was etched on the plaque: "Paul Babcock, who justifies athletics." I was humbled by his words and proud to be thought of in this way. I finally accepted that I was not physically gifted athletically besides my speed. I decided to embrace that fact. I still believed that my heart and determination could help me accomplish anything in life.

It was customary that each player who won an award would say just a few words. When I got to the microphone, I was filled with emotion and said, "Of all the awards that I have received in my life, this is by far the most...*recent*." Luckily, the crowd roared with the laughter for which I was hoping. I heard Arnold Schwarzenegger use this line at an award show and thought it would be perfect to use if I ever got the opportunity. I was relieved that Coach Joe knew how much the award honored me and I would not do anything to lessen the importance of it. The only thing that could match the excitement from the award was that I had just been medically cleared to play. As well as the team was playing, I knew that there was relatively little chance that my role would increase, but at least there was a possibility.

While I was up at the podium, I decided to give Coach Delgado a gift. Coach Del was our third base coach, and it felt like he had to wear a stocking hat all spring since it was so cold. Our "indicator" for signs was the bill of the cap. I cut up one of my old hats and sewed it to a stocking hat so he could properly give signs. It looked ridiculous, but that was the point. I was glad that Coach Del appreciated my sense of humor.

As the NAIA District 20 playoffs began, I felt a level of uncertainty. It was not that I doubted the confidence or ability level of our team. I was simply unsure of how each game would go based on my experiences in the last two years. In the playoffs, any team can win, and it is not always the best team that wins but the team that plays the best. We would have to play our best each game if we were going to advance.

On May 12, we faced Eureka College in game one. It was quite apparent that the playoff energy was cranked up another notch as we catapulted out to an early lead. In the bottom of the eight, I was given an opportunity to hit, and I did not waste any time as the first pitch I saw, I ripped for a double to the left-center gap. I do not think my feet touched the ground until I stood on second. I had spent so much time injured that I had forgotten how good connecting the bat to the ball felt. I drove in the final two runs as we cruised to a 14–0 victory. However, my anxiety level increased because I had seen too many times in sports where a huge offensive output in the first game can lead to an anemic one in the next. We had to turn right around and play conference rival St. Xavier. Fortunately for us, an unearned run early in the game was all fellow captain Ivan Lawler required as he blanked the only team to hand us a loss in a little over a month. That win advanced us to the championship game the next day.

The team that earned their way back to that title game was St. Xavier. We had defeated them three out of the previous four match-ups and were hoping to make it four of five. We did have more wiggle room than they did since it was double elimination, but nobody on our team looked forward to a winner-takes-all scenario. Chovy toed the rubber, equaled the previous pitching performances, and shut the Cougars out. The final score was Saints, 5; Cougars, 0. St. Francis had just advanced to the Great Lakes Region playoffs starting in just six short days.

Another amazing thing about advancing in the playoffs is that final exams are over and most students have left for the summer break. It felt like we were a professional team because our only obligation at that time of year was baseball. With the dorms empty, we only had one another to stay entertained. A few hours a day were spent practicing, and the others we spent horsing around. There is no doubt that our team chemistry increased with each passing day. In previous years, we heard stories of players spraying the fire extinguisher in the hall and playing slip and slide. Luckily as a resident assistant, I did not have to deal with that incident. Our team spent more time hanging out watching movies or playing cards.

The coaches at St. Francis always emphasized the importance of fundamentals. They realized that more games are lost than won. They wanted to make sure that we didn't lose the game because we made careless mistakes. Gordie always preached about muscle memory. If you perform a skill well and do it over and over again, it will become habit. Playoff practices were no different from the regular season. The better part of each practice was spent on throwing, fielding, hitting, and pitching. Every day we would cover what they called IIT, or Individual Improvement Time. We spent fifteen to twenty minutes on the fundamentals of our individual positions. We would then come together for team defense. It always felt like we spent more time on the defensive fundamentals, but I am sure we focused just as much on the offensive side as well. Practices were always well organized, and we got the most out of our time together. Coach made sure that we also scrimmaged to make sure all the hitters and pitchers were in "gamelike" situations.

The weather was as perfect as it could be for those six days. It was a pleasure being outside playing the game we loved. Every day my hand was getting stronger, and I hoped the coaches would see my progress in those practices. I wanted them to know that I was an option if I was ever needed. I was afraid that it would be a catch-22 situation, meaning that if they needed me, more than likely someone on the team was not playing as well as we needed them to play. We were doing well, and maintaining this momentum was more import- ant than playing, even though I wished it could be both.

On May 19, our first opponent of the next round was Aquinas College out of Michigan. I was surprised to discover that I was start- ing in left field since Ivan was on the mound. The six days off did not cause any rust to form on our offensive machine. In our 10–5 win, I contributed an RBI on a bases-loaded walk. It was my third walk of the game. In my last plate appearance, I doubled on the first pitch that I saw. I felt a great personal satisfaction that I could contribute if called upon.

Our second game of the day was against Indiana–Southeast. The phases of the game that we spent so much time on during prac- tice definitely paid off. Our defense and pitching held them to just two runs while our offense generated six runs as we advanced to the championship the next day. This meant we were just one game shy of the World Series. We had been in this position once before when I was a sophomore, but we came up short. It was time to learn from the past and create a new outcome.

The team that advanced to the final game was Ohio Dominican. We again had the comfort of double elimination, but everyone knows how dangerous a winner-takes-all scenario can become. It would be better to dispose of them quickly, and that is exactly what we did. The lead grew to the point that I again got the nod to head to left field and take an at bat. It was like a carbon copy of game one; I lined a double to the gap again on the first pitch. That hit was irrelevant to the outcome of the game, but it reminded me of how fun this game can be. I was also hoping that it left an impression on the coaches. The final score was 10–1, and we could finally say that we were advancing to the NAIA College World Series!

Christie Burke (my resident director) at a graduation party wearing my baseball jacket with my name on the back. She couldn't wait to have it (my name). We started dating after college, and we got married in '96.

Head coach Gordie Gillespie, pitching coach Joe
Heinsen, myself, and assistant coach Tony Delgado
when I received the Joe Heinsen award

Chapter 9

World Series Bound

It is hard to say that there was any disappointment in advancing to the World Series, but for me, there was one. The World Series was held in Des Moines instead of Idaho. The visions that I created in my head from the descriptions of my former teammates were null and void. The experience would be completely different, but truth be told, the only thing that really mattered to us was the outcome, not where it was located.

We had nearly a full week to prepare until we had to leave for Iowa. This week was eerily similar to the previous week. We had great weather, a lot of time to hang out, and plenty of time to practice. Coach Gillespie paid close attention to the details. He knew that our first game was slotted to start at 9:00 a.m. He scheduled each of our practices to start early in the morning so our bodies would be accustomed to this time. I felt like I was a little kid at practice. I was diving around catching looping balls in front of me and to my left and right. It was as if I were back on the farm playing "silo ball." I enjoyed the defensive part of practice as much as the offensive portion. I knew that these would be my last few weeks playing the game I loved, so I might as well give everything that I possibly could.

At practice, I could tell that there was a lighthearted enthusiasm coupled with a seriousness of purpose. The joy of arriving at the field was undeniable, but as practice started, I could feel the shift of our attention to little details. All the players knew what was at stake the following week, and they were determined to give what was necessary. The focus made me believe that my dream was a real possibility. Our shortstop, David Rydberg told our second basemen, Adam VanderWoude, that he was going to tackle him after the last out of the championship game. No one else dared to make a prediction about the World Series.

We spent even more time together because every player was moved to the second floor of Taylor Hall. With all the other students gone, six players, who will remain nameless, drove an old Cadillac from one end of the campus to the other across the quad. They were greeted in the parking lot by the security guard, who simply asked them to park the car and never do that again. Not all players were quite as adventurous. Some guys played darts, while others played RBI baseball on Nintendo. We all seemed to spend a lot of time jammed into a room for four people. Players would be in and out, but everyone was included if we had a ping-pong tournament or some other activity to pass the time. Euchre was played about as much as it was on the bus rides to Texas. I remember thinking that this could be the greatest time of my life and it would have been fun to do this for a profession. We all knew that this was not in the cards for most of us, but at that time, it was everyone's reality.

The night before we were supposed to leave, I went alone to our chapel. This wasn't a typical occurrence for me. I went to mass every Sunday, but I wasn't an overly religious person, and yet there was something telling me to go. The chapel on campus was empty and quiet. I felt a little unsure about the upcoming opportunity, and I needed some time to myself. I was not there to ask God to make all my wishes come true. I was there to ask God to fill a very specific request. My prayer, which came from the depth of my soul, was that Gordie would only play me if it was what was best for the team. I prayed that he would not play me just because I was a senior and a good person. My biggest fear was that he would give me a chance just because I worked my tail off. A small part of me feared that I would blow Gordie's chance at a national title if given a chance. I truly wanted what was best for the team no matter what my role might be.

I was very emotional during this devotional, and all of a sudden, I felt as if I received my answer. My skin was covered with goose bumps, and even though I did not hear the voice of God, I knew he heard me. I left the chapel at peace knowing whatever occurred would be the will of God and I must accept it. It was the most calming experience of my life.

Before we knew it, it was time to load up for our trip. Instead of driving several vans, the school chartered a bus to take us to Des Moines. There was one slight problem as we filled the bus with all our luggage and equipment. There was not enough room for all our stuff in the storage area underneath the bus. I stood next to Gordie and all the bags that would not fit. I could tell that for once, he did not have an immediate solution to our problem. I am not sure where it came from, but I just blurted out, "If you want, I can fit all of this in the bed of my truck, and it has a cap that locks so everything is protected." He looked at me and said, "I will take care of the gas if you wouldn't mind doing that." I pulled my Dodge Dakota up to the pile and loaded it up; everything fit perfectly.

Coach also suggested that I choose a teammate to keep me company. The choice was easy because I spent several road trips sitting next to Jason King. We had a habit of holding odd conversations and making each other laugh with deep thoughts that most other people would find stupid. We discussed our hatred of specific words like *leaflet, pamphlet,* and *brochure.* By no means were these discussions that I had with normal human beings. Quite often we would also partner up when we would hit Wiffle balls. We played a game with each other that when the pitcher gave a signal, we would try to hit a line drive and hit the pitcher. He was much better at hitting me than I was at hitting him.

The drive flew by because we joked around the whole way. We laughed at how random it was that we were riding together while everyone else was stuck on the bus. It was something neither of us could have anticipated when the day started, and we appreciated the strange events that pop up in life. When we arrived in Des Moines, we made a stop at Sec Taylor stadium, the home of the Iowa Cubs, which is the Triple A Affiliate of the Cubs. I think that Gordie wanted us to see the facility that we would be playing in ahead of time so we would not be in awe looking around at our surroundings when we should be focusing on the task at hand. As the team walked around on the field, I cupped my hand to the side of my mouth and yelled, "Hickory!" My teammates immediately got my reference to the iconic movie *Hoosiers*. It was about a small school in Indiana that won the state championship in basketball against a big school. The day before the game, a player yelled that in the gigantic empty gym in which they would play the next night. I wanted my teammates to know that our small school could do the same.

We then took the five-minute drive over to our hotel to unpack and get ready for the World Series Banquet. The purpose of the event was to welcome all eight teams to the tournament and break bread together. It was a formal event, so every player was expected to bring nice clothes. Everyone's definition of "nice clothes" is different, and we discovered that firsthand. I cannot claim that I was in the room, but I have heard the story so many times that it feels like I was there. As players were getting changed, Matt Sisson took one look at Dave DeHaan's outfit and said, "That is not what you are wearing, is it?" Dave was a little stunned by the question because there was nothing he could do about it now since he was hundreds of miles from home. As they came into the lobby to greet the rest of us, Matt loudly announced, "Hey, everyone, the DJ is here." We turned to look and immediately started to roar with laughter. Dave was dressed in what can best be described as a salt-and-pepper MC Hammer ensemble. The pants were a little baggy, the jacket had a few buttons near the navel, and the flared into V cut up the chest. He had a white mock turtleneck on under the jacket. I am sure he felt a little sheepish about wearing it, but he took the teasing like a champ. He knew deep down that we just wanted to give him a hard time. We had grown so close that this brought us even closer.

A nice dinner was immediately followed by some remarks by each of the coaches. There were a total of eight teams, and coincidentally, none of these teams were in attendance the previous year. The teams were Cumberland, Tennessee; Geneva, Pennsylvania; Marion, Wisconsin; Point Loma, California; St. Mary's, Texas; Southeast

Oklahoma, Oklahoma; and Carson–Newman, Tennessee. Based on the length of their messages, I do not think they were given any time restrictions, which was fine because it helped build up the anticipation for when Gordie would speak. Little did we know that he would go last. The message was very similar no matter which representative spoke. The head coach would say how proud he was of his team and all the adversities that they had overcome that season. He talked about their incredible grit and determination. They would tell a few stories about their adventures to arrive at this point. Each coach made it sound like they were the team to beat. The speeches went on for so long it got so hot in the room that Dan Samuilis and Paul Chovanec compared how big their sweat marks were getting after each speaker. Sammy won the battle when his sweat mark actually seeped through the outside of his suit coat. Some of the strangest things entertained us, but they all made us feel like brothers.

When it was Gordie's time to speak, I assumed that he would have a similar message. I could not have been more wrong. He started by congratulating all the teams on their outstanding achievements this season as well as making it to this tournament. He then thanked all the people for their hard work putting everything together, and he knew it was a well-run tournament. Gordie then started talking about how old he and his coaching staff were. He claimed that among the three of them, they must be the oldest staff in the country. He made everyone laugh when he said "We are just happy to be breathing" and "At our age, we don't buy green bananas." Just when I thought it could not become more obscure, he invited up Coach Joe Heinsen and Tony Delgado.

Coach "Del" was wearing a fedora with a little piece of paper placed on the ban that said "Press." He and Joe went right into the Abbott and Costello "who's on first" routine. At this point, I started to look around at my teammates, and they were just as dumbfounded as I was. Their performance went on for what seemed like a long time. They actually did a great job, and we could tell that the other teams were enjoying the novelty of the idea. When they finished, everyone gave them a nice round of applause. I joined in but remembered being disappointed that all the other coaches were bragging about their team and all we got was a comedy routine. What happened next completely changed my perspective. Gordie returned to the podium, again thanked everyone for a great night, and wished all the teams the best of luck. He then very simply yet profoundly pointed at our St. Francis tables and said, "We've got a great team!" Sometimes less really is more. I remember having chills and wanting to start the games immediately.

Unfortunately, the opening ceremony was canceled entirely due to rain. This is where all the teams were paraded onto the field to be introduced. All the seeding of the teams were set along with the game schedule, but the weather needed to cooperate. Since there were eight teams, four games needed to be played on the first day. The forecast showed that the next day could be hit-or-miss as well. We knew we would be playing Point Loma Nazarene from San Diego, California. They were the team who had knocked out Lewis Clark State, who was a perennial power that had won the national championship the last six years. We knew they would be tough whenever game day arrived.

We learned that we were going to attempt to play the next day (May 28) at 9:00 a.m. The bracket predetermined the early slot for us a week earlier. Since our opponent was from California, they had been practicing at 6:30 a.m. to acclimate themselves to the time change. There was no doubt in our minds that their coaches would have them ready for anything. We lost a coin flip, so we would be the visitors and take the first base dugout. We were notified that an early rain would delay our game approximately two hours.

About an hour and a half before game time, our team was found in the parking lot of Sec Taylor stadium. The coaching staff had us divided into groups, and we were hitting Wiffle balls. The team was accustomed to doing this because we all could get a lot of swings in and no time was wasted. Gordie believed that the more repetitions everyone could get, the more muscle memory would work. It was also effective because everyone could throw Wiffle balls without getting a sore arm. We also didn't have to worry about someone getting hurt if they were struck with a ball.

Coach Delgado joked that he had the most important job: keeping the balls from going down the sewer. Coach Del was in the Lewis Athletic Hall of Fame and in his twelfth season coaching at CSF, so he was more than qualified for the job.

I will never forget when our opponent pulled into the parking lot. Their faces were glued to the bus windows. They were gawking at us as if we were zoo animals. As the bus rolled by, I could see every window had at least one player surveying our version of batting practice. I could actually see a few players from the other side of the bus standing in the aisle so they could sneak a peek. I was convinced that they were used to taking BP on the field and this was a foreign concept to them. The rain might stop other teams from batting practice, but it never stopped us.

Chapter 10

Game 1 – Crusaders vs. Saints

The game was being broadcast live on the Joliet radio station, on 1340 a.m. WJOL by Bob Hylka and Dave Laketa. I knew a few people who could not make the four-and-a-half-hour trip who were glad that they could at least listen to the game. Here is a small sample of how I imagined they started the broadcast. This morning, the Crusaders of Point Loma Nazarene will host the Fighting Saints, who will be the visitors on the scoreboard. The Crusaders will be wearing the green jerseys with white letters and numbers as well as white pants and green hats. The Saints are wearing their pinstriped pants to their knees where they have white socks with brown stirrups. The jerseys are brown with gold letters and trim with the corresponding hat. Let's meet the starting lineup for the visitors from Joliet. Leading off and playing shortstop is #5 David Rydberg, who comes in with a 0.306 average. In center field and hitting second, #31 Kerry Paprockas. #15 Ivan Lawler will toe the rubber today and hit for himself in the three hole. Batting cleanup is the first basemen, #14 Dave DeHaan. #33 Brian Guzek will play the hot corner and bat fifth. The second basemen is #11 Adam VanderWoude in the sixth spot. Senior captain and right fielder #12 Dan Samuilis will bat seventh. In the eight hole is the left fielder #18 Paul Babcock. Completing the lineup is the catcher #8 Bob Jones.

That is right; you read it correctly. Gordie must have seen something he liked in the last few games or practices and decided to play me in left field since Ivan Lawler was on the mound. Now it was my job to prove it was not a mistake and help my team win this game. Our pitchers had been doing their part with a team ERA of 2.71. Our offense would get the first at bats against the ace of the Crusader staff. He came in with a team high of seven wins and a 3.91 ERA.

The top of the first started with a two-strike bloop single to center by Rydberg. Anticipating a steal attempt, the pitcher picked to first several times before nearly throwing it away. Paprockas was asked to bunt even though he came in with a team high 0.336 postseason average. Gillespie must have been thinking, *Get him over, get him in for an early lead, and relieve some early pressure.* After bunting two pitches foul, Kerry was asked to bunt again, and this time, he got it down to advance the runner to second. Ivan wasted no time and lined the first pitch to left field for a base hit. The ball was hit so hard that it skipped away from the left fielder, allowing the run to score and Lawler to advance to second. Big games were not unfamiliar to Ivan. When he was a senior in high school, he led St. Catherine's of Racine–Wisconsin to the state title. He was named All-State that year, and that was one of the many reasons Gordie wanted him to attend St. Francis. Several Wisconsin schools were interested in Ivan, including UW Madison, Oshkosh, and Whitewater. He decided to come to CSF after attending a game and visiting with Coach Gillespie. Ivan loved how disciplined and organized the team was under his leadership. He was also impressed by the play of the catcher, Alex Fernandez, and wanted an opportunity to play with him. We were lucky to have Ivan, and he was lucky that he chose CSF because the baseball program in Madison shut down two years later.

The Saints took an early 1–0 lead on the bat of Lawler, who had a team high 46 RBIs. Number 13 John Mika came into run as a courtesy for the pitcher, Lawler. DeHaan took a 1–0 pitch deep off the right field wall for a stand-up RBI double. The Crusaders now trailed 2–0. This was the perfect way to start the World Series for the Saints: get an early lead and put the pressure on the opposition.

DeHaan was stranded at second base after Guzek flied out to center, and VanderWoude "Woody" grounded out to third.

Now it was time for Ivan Lawler to do his thing on the mound. He came into this game winning his last nine starts while throwing eleven complete games with three shutouts. The opposing team batting average against him was just 0.230, and his ERA was 2.04. If those statistics could hold up, another run would look very promising for the Saints. In the bottom of the first, the leadoff hitter ran the count to 3–2. Ivan went to his signature pitch, the forkball, to get a strikeout looking. The following hitter was a lefty who struck out swinging on a 2–2 pitch. Even though Ivan was behind in the count at some point to each hitter, the Crusaders went down 1-2-3 in the first when the three hitter grounded out to second.

The top of the second started with Dan Samuilis "Sammy" falling behind in the count 1–2 and eventually striking out. I came up and tripled down the right field line on the first pitch that I saw. Ambushing the pitcher worked for me in my last two at bats of the playoffs, so I continued that trend. After I dove into third, I gave a little fist punch in celebration. We had a runner at third and only one out. Bob Jones worked the count to 2–2 and roped a double to the gap in right center. We now led 3–0. In an obscure rule, John Mika was able to run for our catcher at second because it was a different inning, but he proceeded to be picked off for out number two. Mika was an all-state baseball player for Driscoll Catholic High School a year ago. He was a significant contributor to state championships in both football and baseball his senior year. He was the quarterback in the fall and a pitcher and outfielder in the spring. Gordie loved to recruit multisport athletes, and John was just that. Rydberg reached on a bobble and a throwing error by the third basemen, but Paprockas erased him on a fielder's choice on the next pitch.

The bottom of the second started with the cleanup hitter taking a 2–2 pitch right back up the middle for a single. After falling behind 3–1, the first basemen blooped a single to right, and with nobody out, the lead runner stopped at second. Trouble was brewing for Ivan and the Saints. The six hitter attempted to sacrifice the two runners over with a bunt, but when he was down two strikes in the count, he lifted a "Texas leaguer" to right. The ball looked like it might be caught, so the runners could only advance one base as the ball fell helplessly among three Saint defenders. The bases were loaded with nobody out. Lawler got ahead of the next hitter, and his 0–2 pitch was scorched down the third baseline, just foul. Two pitches later, he struck out looking on an off-speed pitch. Now a double play could end the inning without any damage, but on the first pitch, the eight hitter drove in a run on a sacrifice fly to center, and the base runner at second advanced to third, barely beating the throw from Paprockas. In limited plate appearances, the next hitter came to the dish with a 0.408 batting average. When the count ran to 3–2, Coach Gillespie made an unexpected trip to the mound. I am not sure what he said, but he probably reminded Ivan that even though this is their nine hitter, he has been their hottest hitter lately and he should not get anything over the middle of the plate. The bases were loaded again with two outs when that hitter took a walk. The lineup rolled over, and on the first pitch, the batter singled to right center. Samuilis cut the ball off and fired it into Rydberg, who turned and threw to the plate to nab the second runner. The inning was over with the Saints holding a 3–2 lead due to some timely defense. If that play was not made, the score would have been tied with runners at the corners with two outs and a 0.301 hitter at the plate.

We needed to get the momentum back and respond with a few runs of our own in the top of the third, and we had our 3-4-5 hitters due up. Ivan drew a walk to start the inning and was replaced by the courtesy runner, Mika. DeHaan fell behind 0–2 but was able to hit the ball on the ground the other way to the shortstop. Fortunately for us, he bobbled the ball and he was unable to get an out with great hustle by the runners. Hoping again to move two runners into scoring position, the next hitter was given the signal to bunt. Guzek's bunt was so awful that it was brilliant. He popped it up over the pitcher's head so he had to reach back awkwardly toward his short-stop. Our runners froze because it appeared as if the ball might be caught. When the pitcher was unable to make the catch, he panicked and threw to first even though he would have had either of the lead runners dead to rights. A hustling Guzek beat the throw to first, and we had bases loaded with nobody out. The opposing coach strolled out to the mound with the intention of having his pitcher minimize the damage and avoid a big inning. Woody came to the plate with a 0.457 average with runners in scoring position but happened to be 0–4 with the bases loaded on the year. He was unable to earn an RBI when he grounded into a 6-4-3 double play, but nonetheless, we extended our lead to 4–2. Sammy worked the count to full before ripping a single up the middle to plate another run and make it a 5–2 ball game. I was shocked when the pitcher grooved another first-pitch fastball to me, and I thanked him by doubling to the left center field gap. Sammy scored to make it 6–2 St. Francis. I was now 2 for 2 with an RBI and a run scored. I was proud to be contributing to our early success. The inning came to a close when Jones nubbed a ball back to the pitcher. Our response to their runs would put the pressure back on Point Loma.

You would think with a four-run lead and two hits in two plate appearances, I would be cool, calm, and collected. I actually did feel good with one exception. I noticed that my right eye unexpectedly began to twitch intermittently. All I could think was, *Don't mess this up for your team, make every play on defense.* In the bottom of the third, Ivan again fell behind the hitter 3–2 before striking him out looking. The next hitter crushed a 2–2 pitch to deep left field near the corner. Luckily, it was hit so high that I was able to camp under it on the warning track just in front of the wall and my eye was kind enough to not spasm in the process. The DH ended the 1-2-3 inning with a harmless pop-up to our second basemen on the outfield grass.

A new pitcher came out to the mound for Point Loma in the top of the fourth inning. He was the opposite of the starter in a few ways. He was a soft-tossing right-hander. Rydberg stayed back on the ball and hit it to the right side, but it was picked up by the first basemen and shoveled to the pitcher covering first. Paprockas followed suit by hitting a rocket the other way to deep short. He was called out on a bang-bang play that the crowd did not agree with. Lawler ended the inning in order by grounding out to short.

Lawler's pitch count continued to rise as he worked behind in the count in the fourth and paid for it when the first hitter drilled a double off the wall in right on a 3–1 count. He advanced to third when the next hitter dribbled the ball up the middle but was extinguished on a nice play by Rydberg. A single up the middle cut the lead to 6–3. Any run scored by the Crusaders tended to increase our team focus. That paid off when the next batter hit a sharp ground ball to third, which Guzek turned into a 5-4-3 inning ending double play.

The Saints went quietly in the top of the fifth even though DeHaan hit a missile to the right fielder on the track and Gooz singled up the middle. The ball did not leave the infield for the next two outs, and the inning was over without a run scoring.

The bottom of the fifth started with the nine hitter grounding to Guzek at third. The play was not close even though the batter dove into first. The top of the order would now be seeing Lawler for the third time. Woody committed his first error in sixteen games on what seemed to be a routine out. He redeemed himself on the next pitch when the two hitter hit a hot shot to his left. Woody spun and started a 4-6-3 double play to end the inning.

I led off the top of the sixth inning and decided to take a new approach and see a pitch from the soft-tossing hurler. After seeing strike one, I decided to lay down a bunt for a hit. However, the pitch nearly hit me, to even the count. I drilled the next pitch between third and short for a sharp single to left. I was now a home run shy of the cycle, a feat that I had never accomplished in my baseball career. The pitcher was obviously concerned that I was going to steal because he threw over four times. After they attempted a pitchout on a 0–1 count, I decided to run on the next pitch. I beat the throw, but my momentum carried me over the bag, and I was not able to maintain the bag with my foot. In the short time that I came off the bag, they were able to tag me out. Jones then hit a high hopper back to the mound for the second out of the inning. Rydberg nearly homered down the left field line, but it was just foul. He was plunked on the next pitch. He then stole second and scored on a single to center by Paprockas, extending the lead to 7–3. Lawler ended the inning with a pop out to short. We seemed to answer every time that they cut into our lead.

Opening the bottom of the sixth inning, the three hitter tried to catch us by surprise and bunt his way on base. He popped the ball up in front of the plate, and Jones pounced on it for an easy out. The cleanup man struck out swinging and was followed by a player who had two hits in two plate appearances against Lawler. This time he grounded sharply to Gooz at third, who bobbled the ball but recovered quickly enough to throw him out to retire the side.

The sky darkened enough that the lights were turned on for the top of the seventh inning, even though it was only midday. DeHaan singled to left to start the frame and was immediately sacrificed to second by Guzek. Before Woody could stride to the plate, the sky opened up and the ground's crew rushed onto the field with tarps for the plate and mound. The teams actually helped put on the full tarp before the infield became too sticky. The rain came down hard for at least twenty minutes. The total delay lasted about an hour, and both teams loosened up again while the ground's crew raked and put the final touches on the field. When we resumed, Coach put on an unusual bunt and run play that was executed well, but Woody was still thrown out at first. We now had a man at third with only one out remaining in the inning. Sammy came through with a two out RBI when he singled to left. This extended our lead to five. I decided try to bunt for a single since I had never hit a home run in college. After my first attempt failed, the third basemen played in, so I decided to swing away. On a two-strike pitch, I launched a lazy fly ball to center to end the inning.

In the bottom half, the leadoff man grounded harmlessly to second before the next two hitters singled to left. Lawler's pitch count was climbing toward the 90 mark, so Coach Gillespie got both a lefty and righty ready in the pen; it was Jason Govert and Ed Young, respectively. The threat was ended when the next hitter spanked a 2–2 pitch right to our third basemen who stepped on the bag and tossed it across the diamond for yet another double play. That was the fourth of the game for the Saints.

Brian Guzek came to CSF as a pitcher and a third basemen. He was voted first-team "all-state" for his high school in Highland, Indiana. As a junior, he was second-team "all-state." What was even more impressive, as a freshman, he led his high school to a second-place finish in football as their quarterback. Gordie loved kids that were athletic enough to play several sports. In fact, the first time he spoke with Gooz on the phone, he offered him a scholarship. Brian was surprised because he had never seen him play. Coach Gillespie told him that he had heard enough about him to know that he would fit right in at CSF. The problem was that Gooz had scholarship offers at St. Joe's, Purdue, and Indiana University. Gordie intrigued him with the possibility of earning playing time as a freshman. Brian decided on St. Francis because the money was right and he hated sitting on the bench. In fact, he gave up pitching because he wanted to play every day. He became our rock at third base.

Jones doubled down the left field line to start our half of the eighth. Rydberg's bunt attempt went right back to the new pitcher who tried to gun down our courtesy runner, Mika, at third, but everyone was safe on the play. Rydberg advanced to second on a ball in the dirt, but the ball was not far enough away for the runner to score from third. On the next pitch, Paprockas hit a comebacker to the pitcher, who looked the runners back but rushed the throw when he saw the speed of Paprockas. He was so fast that the coaches often referred to him as "Bugs Bunny." Two more runs scored on the throwing error, and Paprockas made it all the way to third. Lawler added a single to make the score 11–3. These insurance runs helped ease any tension that may have remained with our club. Billy Phalen was brought on to run for Lawler and was thrown out trying to steal. DeHaan struck out, and Gooz grounded out to close the inning, but the damage was done. We now led by eight runs.

Lawler went back to the mound for the bottom half of the eighth. He coerced the leadoff man to ground to DeHaan at first for an unassisted out. Woody committed his second error of the game by throwing a ball wide of first. We had a habit of "picking each other up" when somebody made a mistake. All good teams find a way to do that. Lawler struck out the next hitter and followed it up by inducing a fielder's choice that went 6–4. The score held at 11–3.

A light rain began to fall in the top of the ninth, but that did not prevent Woody from singling and stealing second. Unfortunately,

Sammy popped out, and I followed with a strikeout. My friend later told me that the announcer proclaimed, "The mighty Casey has struck out." Coach sent up pinch hitter Brian Olson to the plate for Bob Jones. On most occasions, Brian was our left-handed designated hitter when Lawler played left field. I am sure Coach wanted to keep him sharp for the next game. He flew out to right to end yet another threat. Three defensive outs to go.

Ivan Lawler trotted back out to the mound to go for his twelfth win of the season. He looked sharper in the ninth than he did in the early innings. Out number one came on a checked-swing strikeout. Out number two came on a fly out to center on a 1–2 pitch. Three up and three down when the next hitter grounded into a 5–3 put-out. A complete game was in the books for Ivan Lawler. The Saints scored eleven runs on seventeen hits, while the Crusaders managed just three runs on eight hits. If anyone on the team doubted Coach Gillespie's methods, they must have been put to rest by that offensive barrage. The Wiffle balls served us better than batting practice on the field.

I later discovered that the broadcast team named me the player of the game. Quite an honor for someone who could have given up when he was told, "You will never play here." The truth was clear to me; I would not be in this position if it were not for those words. I worked harder than I thought possible because I had something to prove. If it wasn't for Coach Delgado's message from the coaching staff, I may have never made myself good enough to play. However, there was still more work to be done.

Of course, my parents were in the crowd, joined by my sister Louise. They made it sound like someone different from the family was going to try to join my parents every day. We also discovered that when the location changed, so did the number of teams in the tournament. When Lewis Clark State was the host, they received an automatic bid, and then an at-large bid was added to make a total of ten teams. There were only eight teams in this tournament, and we would play the winner of the next game between St. Mary's and Geneva.

My parents had proof for my siblings that I was in the lineup.

Chapter 11

Game 2 — Golden Tornados vs. Saints

The Rattlers of St. Mary's were initially the number 1 seed in the tournament. However, they were eliminated when they lost to Point Loma in the first game of day 2. On day 1, they were upset by the number 8 seed, Geneva, in their first game of the tournament, showing once again that anything can happen in baseball. We now faced Geneva, who came in with a team ERA of 2.50, which was slightly better than our 2.71. We were the home team in this game but continued to wear the same uniform as the day before. The Tornados' uniforms were unusual because both their jerseys and pants were black with gold trim, letters, and numbers. Their school was located in Beaver Falls, Pennsylvania.

The pitching matchup was another lefty for the Tornados, who came in with a 2.45 ERA against our right-handed Paul Chovanec, who was 12–0 on the season. On paper, it would appear that this would be a low-scoring affair. Joining my parents was my Uncle Bob Babcock, who was a tank driver during the Battle of the Bulge during World War II. They settled into their seats just as we took the field as the home team.

The leadoff man for Geneva in the bottom of the first was a speedster who had thirty-one stolen bases on the year. Chovy kept him off the base paths in his first plate appearance by striking him out. Unfortunately, Paul fell behind the next two hitters and issued two free passes to create immediate trouble for the Saints. The threat was eliminated when the cleanup hitter bounced into a 4-6-3 inning ending double play. This was already our sixth double play of the young tournament.

The only change in the lineup for Coach Gillespie was that Ivan Lawler would DH for the pitcher Chovanec. I probably remained in my spot because there was a lefty on the mound and our regular DH was also left-handed. It is also possible that Coach wanted to rest Ivan's arm. The final reason could be that I played well enough in the first game that he thought I could help the team.

Rydberg flew out deep to center to start the bottom of the first for us. Paprockas followed with a shot up the middle. He stole second on the next pitch without a throw since the catcher had to block the pitch in the dirt. Ivan now had an opportunity to drive in the first run of the game two days in a row. He hit a looping liner into right center that was caught by a diving right fielder. The runner could not advance on the play. DeHaan worked the count to full before drawing the base on balls. Brian Guzek came to the plate with a 0.360 batting average when there are two outs and runners in scoring position. Unfortunately, he struck out on a ball in the dirt, and the catcher was able to cut him down before he reached first. No score at the end of the first.

The visitors' half of the second started with a player who had two RBIs yesterday and a total of thirty-three on the year. Chovy got ahead in the count 0–2 but ran the count to full before issuing another free pass. The next hitter scorched a sinking line drive to left field that I awkwardly dove forward for and caught for the first out of the inning. My eye started to twitch again as I tossed the ball into the cutoff man. The second out came on the very next pitch on a pop out to shortstop on the outfield grass. As the lefty designated hitter worked the count to 2–2, the courtesy runner for their catcher stole second to move into scoring position. Chovy then issued his fourth walk of the day. Any player will tell you that laws of baseball are bound to catch up with you when you don't play it the right way. Walks and errors tend to come around to score when you continue to test fate. Luckily for us, that did not happen in this inning as the

Tornados' threat ended when their nine hitter took a called third strike.

VanderWoude led off our half of the frame with a walk. He stole second on the first pitch to Samuilis, who eventually walked as well. I strolled to the plate in an obvious bunting situation. Before I knew it, I had bunted the first two pitches foul. The St. Francis way was all about "old-school" baseball and executing, so I was expected to get a bunt down with two strikes. Unfortunately, I could not keep that bunt attempt fair either, and it was a K (strikeout) in the scorebook. Coach Gillespie had little patience for a lack of execution. I walked to the dugout hoping my teammates could pick up my slack. Bob Jones followed me with a grounder to short that only went as a fielder's choice because he avoided the double play by beating the throw by hustling to first. John Mika then ran for him so he could get his catcher's gear on. Dave Rydberg smoked a single to left, and the dreaded leadoff walk scored the first run of the game. Gordie always taught us to hustle and that run was the reward; if Jones didn't hustle down the line, the inning ends without a run because of a double play. "It doesn't take talent to hustle" was a common rally cry of the coaches and we bought in. Mika and Rydberg were stranded when Paprockas harmlessly grounded to first, but the Saints scored first and led 1–0.

The top of the order was up again as Chovy started the top of the third. He struck out the leadoff man for the second time on the day. The next hitter grounded out to short for the second out of the inning. The next pitch was clubbed over my head, and I slipped down as I turned to track down the ball. Just before I recovered, the ball short-hopped the wall and bounced back toward the infield; our center fielder picked it up and held him to a double. The cleanup hitter worked a full count but ended the inning with a ground ball to second, so no damage was done.

Their lefty settled in with his first 1-2-3 inning of the game by striking out both Lawler and DeHaan to start the frame. Guzek grounded out to shortstop, and the home half of the third was in the books. Paul Chovanec responded with a quick inning of his own by getting a fly out and two groundouts in the top of the fourth. It was only a fluke that brought Chovy to St. Francis. Coach Del and Gordie were recruiting another player in Hoffman Estates when they saw Paul warming up in the bullpen. Gordie later told the papers, "There was something about that big awkward kid that intrigued me." Paul had planned on going to Kishwaukee Community College before he spoke with Gordie and went on a visit. Chovy committed to CSF after spending more time with the coaching staff. They created an environment that made their players feel comfortable.

Woody struck out swinging to start our half of the fourth. This was unusual for him because he was normally a great offensive player. He hit 0.507 in his senior year at T. F. South High School to set their high watermark. He was such a good student in high school that he received baseball offers from Notre Dame, Northwestern, and Xavier University. He ended up at St. Francis because Gordie told him that he would have an opportunity to play right away. Ninety percent of his education would have been paid for at Xavier University, but he and his father felt more comfortable with seeing playing time right away, and they loved how the coaches seemed like another set of parents. We were lucky to have him as a part of our young infield.

Sammy continued the inning by doubling all the way to the wall in right center on a 3–1 pitch; he thought about going for third but thought better of it and slammed on the brakes and returned to second. I took a four-pitch walk to give us runners at first and second with one out. Jones flew out to center, but it was not deep enough for either of us to advance. Geneva avoided a big inning when Rydberg grounded into a 6–4 fielder's choice. We headed into the fifth with the score remaining 1–0.

Both pitchers went into shutdown mode in the fifth. Chovy recorded two more groundouts and a strikeout in the top half. The bottom went just as quickly as their pitcher induced a pop out and two groundouts.

The heart of the Geneva order was due up in the top of the sixth. Chovy showed some displeasure with the umpire when the count went to 2–0; that normally leads to trouble with the officiating crew. Very rarely will a pitcher get the next close call, and as predicted, the count went to 3–0. Chovy battled back to make it a full count but eventually walked the leadoff man. Baseball statistics have shown that when the leadoff runner gets on, the scoring percentages increase dramatically. We hoped we could avoid that trend here. Their three hitter hit a bullet line drive to short for an out, but Rydberg was unable to double off the quick reaction of the base runner. The cleanup man took the next pitch and split the gap between Paprockas and myself in left center field. I played the ball off the wall and relayed it to Rydberg, but the throw was too late to the plate, and the score was knotted at 1–1 with the go-ahead run at second. Even though it was only the second hit of the game off Chovanec, Gordie strolled out to the mound, and Young and Govert got loose again in the bullpen. After the quick visit, the five hitter took a 2–2 pitch to deep left, but I was able to camp under it and gather some momentum for the throw to third. The base runner held up, but my eye continued to twitch. The fact that I feared my twitching eye would negatively impact the series at some point probably made it worse. I actually liked the way it felt, but it did annoy me that it seemed to act up only when the ball was hit in my general direction. The go-ahead run was stranded at second when the next batter grounded out to second.

If momentum can change, I would say it changed in the bottom of the sixth. Our first two hitters forced the count to full but then struck out, one swinging and the other looking. Sammy hit a Sunday hop to the shortstop, and it was three up and three down for the Saints with the score tied.

Chovy faced the bottom of their order to start the seventh and quickly got ahead in the count 0–2. The freshman second basemen / closer battled back to draw the dreaded leadoff walk. The next hitter had every intention on sacrificing his teammate over to second with a bunt but pulled the bat back three times for a 3–0 count. On the fourth pitch, he threw his bat toward the dugout anticipating a ball four call. He was mistaken and had to sheepishly return to the box. Unfortunately, the next pitch was not close enough for the umpire to call it a strike. Now the nine hitter came up in another clear bunting situation, runners at first and second and zero outs. He got the first pitch down, and DeHaan pounced on it immediately and threw to third. The runner at second got an even better jump and beat the force at third on a bang-bang play. The bases were now loaded, and there was still nobody out. Our infielders were now playing near the edge of the grass so they could get a force out at the plate. The lead-off man floated a 1–1 pitch down the line in shallow right. Sammy raced over, but the ball fell just out of his reach about ten feet inside the line. Each base runner advanced only ninety feet since it looked like the ball might be caught. We now trailed 2–1, and the bags were still jammed with no one out. The next pitch was drilled on the ground to third, Guzek threw home for one, and Jones threw to first for the 5-2-3 double play. Now runners were at second and third with two outs. The next hitter was the 1993 offensive player of the year in District 18, but he was facing the district 6 pitcher of the year. Chovanec's ERA was an outstanding 1.59 for the year. This was exactly what both teams wanted. I apparently was not playing deep enough because he hit another ball over my head that I played off the wall and relayed to Rydberg, hoping to prevent an extra run from scoring. Rydberg realized that we had no chance to get either man at home, and he threw to Woody, covering the bag at second to get the final out of the inning. The damage was done, three runs crossed the plate, and we now trailed 4–1 heading into the bottom of the seventh. Three of their four runs originated via the base on balls. Our record on the year when trailing after six innings was a miserable 5–14, and we had the bottom of our order coming up.

My place in the order was due up for the bottom of the seventh inning. The only thing I was thinking while striding to the plate was, *Don't try to do too much. Your team needs you on base, only swing at your pitch a fastball down the middle.* I took the first pitch up and away. The pitcher evened the count on a fastball low and away on the outside corner. The count again turned in my favor when he missed down in the zone. I knew that most pitchers feel more stress when behind in the count, and I knew how comfortable I felt when ahead in the count. The next pitch came at me in slow motion and looked like a watermelon. I hit a ball high and deep off the Coke sign on the top of the wall in left field for a stand-up double. If the fence were not so high, I would have had my first college home run. We were now in business. Bob Jones worked the count to 2–0, and the opposing coach decided to make a change. The new pitcher came into this game with a 6–0 record and a 1.45 ERA. He also had 42 Ks with only 4 BB. He inherited the 2–0 count on Jones and walked him within three pitches. By rule, the walk was charged to the starter. We were now back to the top of our lineup. Rydberg hit a deep fly ball to center just shy of the track. I decided to tag and go for third. The throw short-hopped the third basemen as I dove in safely and Mika advanced to second running for Jones. Now we had two runners in scoring position and just one out. Luckily, my risky base running worked to our advantage. Paprockas was given the green light even though many times Gordie would put us into "plus one." This means that hitters take a pitch until they get a strike and in a 3–1 count as well. I am sure Gordie knew that this pitcher was always around the zone and he turned the top hitters loose. Paprockas scorched a line drive right at the third basemen. I was taking our normal walking lead from third as the ball hit his glove. I should have been dead to rights, but he glanced at me as the ball hit his glove, and he dropped it. I dove back in safely. His throw was late to first since he tried to tag me. The bases were loaded with one out. I wondered what would have happened if I did not tag up and advance to third on the previous fly ball. Would the third basemen have turned that line drive into a double play without me in his line of sight at third? I was just thankful that the inning continued.

Even though Ivan was 0–3 on the day, he was the guy we wanted in the batter's box. He had driven in the most runs on our team this year. The pitcher must have been aware of this because he was trying to work the edges of the zone and got behind 3–1. Ivan hit a fly ball to right, so I went back to the bag to tag up. The right fielder appeared to be settling under the ball, but it miraculously bounced right out of his glove, and everyone moved up a base. There was no logical explanation of why he dropped it, but we were gaining momentum because of it. We still trailed 4–2, but the go-ahead run was now at first. We all hoped Dave DeHaan would live up to his "cleanup man" spot in the lineup. On a 1–1 pitch, Dave hit a rocket the other way, splitting the left center field gap. One run scored, two runs scored, Lawler came all the way around from first to score as DeHaan slid into third with his first triple of the year.

The Fighting Saints media guide had an interesting quote about Dave from Gordie: "A guy who can help win us a national championship." Dave came from Andrew High School, where he became the school's first four-year starter on the varsity in baseball. Gordie knew how good of an athlete he was because he was also a three-year starter in basketball. Gordie was building a team full of solid athletes like Dave DeHaan. We hoped his "prediction" would come true; for the moment, he looked like Nostradamus.

The Saints took the lead 5–4 and still had a runner at third with only one out. The Tornados brought in their infield to try to cut down a runner at the plate. That move was not needed as Guzek struck out for the third time. The inning ended when VanderWoude smoked a line drive right at the shortstop. We responded with a big inning of our own, took the momentum back, and now just needed to hold on to the lead. Baseball is such a crazy game. I often wondered how different the inning might have been if my ball left the ballpark for a home run. I was starting to think it was destiny.

Chovy went back out to the mound with a renewed sense of purpose. He got the first out by inducing a ground ball to the right side. DeHaan fielded it cleanly and tossed it to Chovy covering the bag. He fell behind the next hitter 3–1 but forced a pop out to our shortstop. It only took two more pitches to get a comebacker that Chovy shoveled to first for a welcomed 1-2-3 inning. He only needed three defensive outs to achieve his thirteenth victory on the year.

Sammy started the bottom half of the eighth by working the count to full after being behind 0–2. He hit a bullet to the shortstop, who made a nice play to throw him out. That reminded me of a time early in the year when Sammy came back to the dugout very frustrated after hitting a ball well but making an out. He was complaining about how he could not catch a break and, even though he was not striking out, balls were not falling for him. He used the Lord's name in vain and said, "I give up. God, if you just let me get a hit in my next at bat, I will go to church every Sunday for the rest of the season." He shook his head in disbelief after his next plate appearance

153

when he hit a home run. I know Sammy made good on his promise because I saw him at mass each week. We even found a church in Des Moines during the World Series so he could stay true to his word.

I saw three straight balls to start my at bat but then took three straight strikes expecting to draw a walk. It appeared that the inning would be over when Jones hit a ground ball to second, but a wild throw allowed him to reach. He was lifted for Mika to run. Rydberg ambushed the first pitch and doubled in a key insurance run, making it 6–4. Five of the six runs that we scored so far were unearned. The inning ended when Paprockas grounded to the first baseman for an unassisted out.

Chovy returned to the mound trying to match Lawler with a complete game of his own. Even though he was facing the bottom third of the order, he fell behind 3–1 to the first hitter of the ninth inning. The next ball was shot down the third baseline but back-handed cleanly by Gooz as his toss across was in time for out number one. It was the first at bat of the day for the next hitter who came in during the Tornado pitching change. He rifled a ball that was ticketed to right but was stopped by an amazing play by VanderWoude diving to his left, contorting his body with his glove above his head, two down. The final chance for Geneva came down to a pinch hitter. On Chovanec's 144th pitch, the game was over via the strikeout.

We scored six runs on six hits while committing no errors. The Golden Tornados scored four runs on four hits but committed three costly errors. The player of the game was Dave DeHaan for his critical three-run go-ahead triple. The Saints stayed in the winner's bracket and awaited their next opponent. Later on, Chovy confided in me that he thought he blew it and let us all down. He was so happy that the offense bailed him out with a great comeback.

After the game, Woody felt a tug on his jersey. He turned around and saw a young boy with a ball. The boy said, "My name is Adam too, I saw that great play you made. Could I have your autograph?" Woody could not believe his ears; with a huge smile, he bent down and had a quick talk with the boy as he signed his ball. The youngster got quite a thrill but had no idea how thrilled he made Woody.

"Chovy" with pitching coach Joe Heinsen after the game

Chapter 12

Game 3 — Saints vs. Savages

Our next foe was very familiar because we had traveled to Durant, Oklahoma, the last several years during our spring trip. This year, we dropped a doubleheader to the Savages of Southeastern Oklahoma State. We were hoping that trend would not continue, but we were a much different team now, but I am sure they were as well. A few of their most famous graduates were Dennis Rodman of the Detroit Pistons and Brett Butler of the Los Angeles Dodgers.

Scott Slocum joined Dave Laketa in the radio booth, replacing Bob Hylka. The Savages were the visitors and facing our freshman left-handed pitcher, Steve Ochman. In his first two playoff appearances, he only allowed one run for an ERA of 0.50. His ERA for the year was second on the team at 1.73. This was a promising trend since his earned run average in high school was 0.72. Our lineup remained the same except for the fact that Lawler went to right field and Sammy became the DH. We were facing yet another lefty, so I remained in the lineup as well. That was great news for my sister Patti, who drove over with her husband, Mike. My parents were busy keeping everyone else in the family updated on our success thus far and intent on getting as many family members to a game as possible.

In the bull pen before the game, Chovy thought he would have a little fun with our rookie starting pitcher. He commented on how big the Savage lineup was and how they looked like they could kill us. Steve just laughed and told him where he could "go." This was typical behavior of the senior captain. He loved keeping people loose by exaggerating how good the other team was. He assured Steve that he should trust his "stuff" and he would be just fine. All year long, Paul had taken him under his wing, and he was there again to calm his nerves before the biggest game of his life.

Steve Ochman got ahead early in the count to the first hitter before slipping to a full count. He froze the hitter with a fastball on the inside corner resulting in a strikeout even though the hitter started running to first like it was ball four. The next hitter also ran the count to full before fisting a ball to short. Dave Rydberg reacted quickly and made a nice play, but the umpire signaled safe, much to the disappointment of at least half the crowd. The next pitch was lifted harmlessly to center field for the second out. The cleanup man hit a ball up the middle that would have been a hit, but the runner was stealing, and that forced our second basemen to cover. The ball went right into his glove as he stood on the bag for a force out to end the first.

For the third consecutive game, we faced a lefty on the mound. He came in with a 7–0 record and an ERA of 3.12. People crunching the numbers might say that we had the advantage, but the numbers do not play the game; if they did, we would not have rallied to win the last game. Rydberg started the home half of the first with a one-hop shot at the third basemen. He made a great stab at the ball, and his throw in the dirt was picked by the first baseman. Paprockas was caught looking after running the count to full. The first ended without a run when Lawler hit a bullet on 0–2 to deep right field, but the right fielder was in perfect position to make the play.

The top of the second started with a deep fly to center, but our fleet-footed center fielder tracked it down. After making the catch, he slipped down due to all the rain that we had gotten over the last several days. All the games were played, and the field was in great shape, considering what transpired. There were just a few areas in the outfield that remained slick. The outfield had a great drainage system, but the water from the full infield tarp was dragged onto the outfield grass. All the outfielders were aware of the conditions. The next two batters struck out swinging to create Ochman's first 1-2-3 inning.

The second inning started with the hero from the day before, but DeHaan struck out swinging this time. The second out of the inning came on a tapper back to the mound by Guzek. Woody followed with a sharp single. He attempted to steal when Samuilis hit the first pitch a mile, but it was well foul down the line in left. It was a shame because Woody had the bag stolen easily. The Savages called for a pitchout, but there was nothing doing. Anticipating that they would not pitch out twice in a row, Woody was off to the races, and the throw went into center, but he was unable to advance to third since the center fielder did a nice job of backing up. Samuilis was issued a walk a few pitches later. I came up with two outs and runners in scoring position. My season average in this spot was 0.429 in limited opportunities. I worked the count to full but struck out swinging on a nasty curveball.

Ochman started the third with two more strikeouts, which made four in a row and totaled five for the game. The side was retired on a sky-high fly out to center. It was still a scoreless game in the middle of the third. Brian Guzek was the main reason Steve ended up at St. Francis. He had narrowed his options down to CSF and Valpraiso University in Indiana. Gooz's and Steve's backyards were right next to each other, and they were teammates two years ago at Highland High School. Brian shared how much he enjoyed his first year and convinced him that we could be really good if he joined us in Joliet. Valpo had single-digit wins the year before, so Steve decided to become a Saint.

Our half of the inning started with Jones bouncing out to second. He was followed by Rydberg, who singled sharply to left on the first pitch. Many of Dave's hits so far in the series were early in the count. Luckily, the opponents had not scouted this. He immediately swiped second and just barely beat the throw. Paprockas hit a ball up the middle that the second basemen tried to backhand. It was ruled an error when it went under his glove and Rydberg came around to score in the process. On the throw home, Paprockas advanced to second. Ivan then hit a bullet to left. Coach Delgado decided to wave in the speedy Paprockas, and he scored when the throw was up the line, which, in turn, allowed Ivan to advance into scoring position as well. Saints led 2–0. DeHaan popped out in foul ground to the catcher. With two strikes and two outs, Brian Guzek singled to right to bring in Lawler, extending the lead to three.

The Savages' coach decided to make a pitching change after that third run of the inning. He brought in a right-handed pitcher, who hit VanderWoude in the face with a curveball on only his second pitch. There was great confusion in our dugout for the next several minutes. We watched Coach Gillespie and the medical staff rush to Woody's side. For a few moments, we did not see any movement. All of a sudden, VanderWoude got up and, with an angry demeanor, headed to the dugout with the medical staff. He was slapping five with teammates on his way into the dugout. Even though Jason Jonas was sent to first to run for him, Coach Gillespie was meeting with the home plate umpire to discuss the situation. A few moments later, Woody appeared from the dugout and hustled down to first to run for himself. All his teammates and the crowd were both impressed and inspired by his toughness.

Adam VanderWoude was a physical specimen who had very little body fat. In fact, a younger baseball player asked other players how he got such great abdominal muscles. That gave Matt Sisson an idea. He told Woody to rub Noxema on his stomach after he was done shaving in the bathroom. The other player witnessed this and went right out and bought a bunch of Noxema. Sure enough, the next day, players saw the younger player slathering it all over his abs. Everyone except him was in on the joke. Playing pranks on people always brought us closer together.

Sammy continued the inning by drawing a walk to load the bases for yours truly. The pitcher got ahead of me, and on a 1–2 count, I knew we could not afford for me to strike out again. I just wanted to give us a chance by putting the ball in play. I was able to see the ball a little deeper in the zone and hit a hard ground ball toward second. The ball kicked up on him and headed into right center. Two more runs scored on his second error of the inning. Bob Jones then split the gap in left center field. Sammy scored easily from third, and since there were two outs, I motored all the way around from first, making it 7–0. Rydberg was hit by a pitch to give us runners at first and second with two outs. With no lead being comfortable, we successfully completed a double steal. Some coaches may frown upon this with a sizable lead, but Coach Gillespie saw it as the most sincere compliment. He was showing other coaches that we would continue to play hard because the other team is good enough to come back and win. Coach would call off play that is more aggressive if the score got out of hand, but we were only in the third inning. There was a lot of baseball still to be played. The Savages again changed pitchers, and this one successfully ended the inning with a 4–3 putout.

Ochman sailed along in the fourth. Sandwiched between two fly outs, he did give up a single to left. The runner never made it any further when he struck out the next hitter. We treated him like every other starting pitcher who was in a groove; we left him alone and didn't talk to him. Our half of the inning started with a single past the second basemen on a play that we believed his counterpart would have made. DeHaan struck out on three pitches, and Guzek popped out to the catcher trying to bunt for a hit. Woody hit a slow roller to short who booted it, so everyone was safe. The scoring threat ended when Sammy grounded out to second.

The fifth inning started harmlessly with a pop out to shallow right; however, the mood changed quickly when the seventh hitter in the order singled to left. Ochman then had trouble finding the plate for the bottom two hitters in the lineup. The back-to-back walks loaded the bases with only one out. Gordie took a trip to the mound as Ed Young started to get loose in the bull pen. Steve Ochman knew that this would be a short outing if he did not get out of this jam quickly. The Savages were now back to the top of the order. The leadoff hitter was 0 for 2 on the day and had committed two costly errors at second base. He was looking for redemption in this plate appearance. He knew with one swing of the bat the complexion of the game could change completely. His luck did not improve, however, when he popped out in foul ground to DeHaan near first. The drama ended a few pitches later when the next hitter also popped out in foul territory.

In the bottom half of the inning, I continued the streak of popping the ball up for an out. Their second basemen continued his horrendous game by committing his third error of the game on a ball hit by Rydberg. His fourth error was avoided when his first basemen scooped his errant throw on a double play to end the inning.

The sixth, seventh, and eighth innings flew by with relatively little action that resulted in no runs for either team. Steve Ochman went out to the mound in the ninth looking to surpass the performances of both Lawler and Chovanec. They both went the distance but were unable to shut out the opposing team. Steve was able to hit most of his spots because he trusted in the pitches that Bob Jones was calling. Everything was clicking for the young man as he pounded the glove pitch after pitch. The freshman looked stronger in the ninth and disposed of the Savages easily with a three-up and three-down inning. He finished the game the same way he started it, with a strikeout. This was the first time that the Savages were shut out all year long. We became the only remaining undefeated team in the tournament with a perfect 3–0 record.

Ivan Lawler was named the player of the game with three hits and an RBI. We were now scheduled to play the next night at 7:00 p.m. against Cumberland University. After the game, the team went to Hyvee. This restaurant does not exist in Illinois, but our coaches fell in love with it, and it felt like we ate every meal there. The only meal that we did not have at this establishment was when the host school took us out to an Italian restaurant. Hyvee is a store that sells just about everything under the sun but also has a cafeteria area. It took us a few days to figure out that we could order individual omelets. We did not complain about going there all the time because there were a variety of choices, but more importantly, the team who won the national championship the year before frequently ate there. We continued the trend of being superstitious baseball players.

That night, I decided to visit the Laundromat because my uniform was filthy. We had worn the same uniform for the first three games. I was not so superstitious that I thought the good luck would be washed away. Since I was a captain, I told everyone on the team that I would take their uniforms as well. I did make an underclassman (John Mika) come with me so I did not have to do everything by myself. As we sat around talking about how much fun the season has been, he looked at me and said, "You have really been the man in the World Series." I just laughed and told him I was so glad to get the opportunity and help the team. That was always my goal, and it was not going to change now. I knew that in baseball, past success did not always indicate future success. In addition, I was still superstitious enough that I did not want to jinx anything that I had going.

When we returned to the hotel, we ran into Coach Blaylock in the lobby. He relayed this story to us. He saw a Savage player using the pay phone and heard him say the following to his father: "I can't believe that we lost, but not only that, we got shut out by a *freshman.*" Our team was even being talked about in Oklahoma.

Chapter 13

Game 4 — Saints vs. Bulldogs

Cumberland University was a very dangerous team to play because they led all tournament teams in most offensive categories. They were very well-balanced and athletic, which their 75 home runs and 108 stolen bases could measure. We lost to them 6–3 when we faced them earlier in the year. They were even more dangerous because they were one game from elimination.

If they won this matchup, they would play Southeastern Oklahoma the next day and we would have a bye. If we won, we would play the Savages for the title at two o'clock the following day. That time needed to be moved up due to the weather forecast. The rain had been hit-or-miss all tournament long, so why would things change now? The weather that night was unseasonably cool with another chance of rain later. I was sure the Bulldogs from Lebanon, Tennessee, would have preferred warmer weather, along with all the fans who were settling in for the nightcap. My brother Dick drove over with his wife, Neva, to join my parents, who became the unofficial welcoming crew to Saints fans.

The Bulldogs were wearing all white uniforms with maroon letters and numbers as well as maroon sleeves underneath. We decided to stay with the same uniforms. I was sure that someone would give me a hard time if our clean uniforms were on the losing end.

The starting pitcher was the fourth lefty in a row that we would face. He came in with a 9–4 record and a 2.39 ERA on the year, but he faced Ivan Lawler, who came in with a 2.11 ERA and an extended winning streak and twelve complete games to his credit. That meant that Samuilis was back in right, and Bob Jones and I flip-flopped spots in the batting order. We were first up since we were the visitors on the scoreboard.

Rydberg took the first pitch that he saw and lifted a fly ball to center for the first out of the game. Kerry Paprockas worked a big part of his game by showing bunt again but pulled back for a called strike. He had been showing bunt more often in the series since he was facing so many lefties. In general, lefty hitters have a harder time against a lefty pitcher because their off-speed pitches break away from the hitter. He then grounded a ball to short that was mishandled, and they had no chance to get the speedy center fielder. I took great pride in being the fastest man on the team, but I must admit that both Paprockas and VanderWoude gave me a run for my money and might have surpassed me. Our team speed definitely made us an athletic group as well. The aggressive Ivan Lawler hit the first pitch to second, which led to a 4-6-3 inning ending double play.

Lawler returned to the mound hoping to continue the effectiveness of the Saints' pitching staff. The leadoff man hit a hot shot to short that was gloved and thrown across for out number one. The next ball was hit sharply down the line and backhanded by Brian Guzek, who threw late to first; however, the umpire signaled foul, so we had to do it again. The next pitch was popped into foul ground down the right field line for the second out of the inning. The bulldog three hitter came into the game with fourteen home runs and ninety-one RBIs on the season. Lawler missed with four straight to give the bulldogs their first base runner of the game. The inning ended with Ivan's first strikeout of the game.

Our cleanup man showed that the opponent must stay awake for every hitter as he attempted a bunt for a hit. Everyone in the lineup had attempted a bunt for a hit at some point in the tournament so the opposition could not take it for granted. Unfortunately, no one had successfully executed it so far, and DeHaan finished his at bat with a strikeout, so that streak continued as well. Gooz singled sharply to left. Woody hit a ball high and deep to left that Guzek went halfway to second on but then retreated when the ball was caught. The inning ended with Sammy grounding out to second.

The bottom of the second began with a little nubber out in front of the mound. Ivan pounced on it and barely nabbed the runner at first. The next hitter took a 1–2 curveball and singled into right. Lawler tried to keep the runner honest by throwing over four times because he had thirty-seven stolen bases on the year. The runner broke for second, but the ball was fouled out of play. The next pitch was a hard shot to Guzek, but it bounced off his shoulder and ricocheted to Rydberg near the infield grass by shortstop; he faked a throw to first but gave a quick throw to Woody covering second, expecting a double-play opportunity. Rydberg caught the lead runner in a rundown when he rounded the bag on the fake to first. A wild play and base-running miscue led to another out for the Saints. When the count went to full on the lefty designated hitter, DeHaan played behind the runner to give himself some more range. It did not matter as he took ball four to put runners at first and second with two outs. The nine hitter ended the threat with a Sunday hop to short.

Both pitchers settled in for the next two innings, and each retired the next six hitters in order. Needless to say, the third and fourth innings flew by. Our top half of the fifth started with Guzek. He came into the game with a 0.488 OBP and continued that trend with his forty-third base on balls of the year. Adam VanderWoude took ball one before laying down a beautiful bunt. The defense made a great play to barely get him at first. Guzek had to hold at second when Dan Sumuilis hit the first pitch to shortstop. Bob Jones then singled to right, and Coach Del waved Gooz around third. I left my spot in the on deck circle to motion a slide away from the plate, which he executed perfectly, but the umpire called him out to end the inning. It was a perfect one-hop throw by the right fielder. His teammates poured out of the dugout to congratulate him. We hoped this spectacular play would not lead to instant offense for the Bulldogs.

The bottom of the fifth started with a leadoff double to the gap in left center. Woody and Lawler then ran a pickoff play to second; it was a close play, but the runner was called safe. The next pitch bounded up the middle; VanderWoude charged and decided to use his momentum and throw to third where Guzek tagged out the lead runner. It was great anticipation by Woody, who took a runner out of scoring position. That play loomed large because the next player had a base hit to right, which would have easily scored the run. The Bulldogs still had runners at first and third with only one out. The bags were jammed as soon as Lawler hit the next batter. Lawler decided to fake to third and throw to first. The oldest trick in the book worked, and he caught the runner at first in a rundown. DeHaan threw to Woody, but the base runner returned to first harmlessly when Lawler failed to cover the bag. A wasted opportunity by the Saints. The bases were still loaded with only one out. Lawler then induced a ground ball to third, Gooz came home for one, and Jones's throw to first was not in time. Two outs with the bases still jammed, for the Bulldogs leading RBI man due up. He had come through in so many big spots earlier in the year that he was exactly who they wanted at the dish. Luckily, he stranded the three runners as he grounded out to second base. Somehow, Lawler and the Saints were able to avoid a disastrous inning.

An uneventful sixth inning came and went without any damage for either team. The Bulldog pitcher continued to dominate our lineup in the top of the seventh as well. The bottom half of their inning started with a single to left. The next hitter struck out looking after failing twice to advance the runner with a sacrifice bunt. That was a critical play since the following hitter singled to give them runners at first and second with one out. A line drive to center looked like trouble, but the ball stayed elevated long enough for Paprockas to make a nice catch for the second out of the inning. The very next pitch was ticketed for left field, but Rydberg dove to keep it on the infield. He threw to third hoping to catch the runner rounding third to no avail. This play more than likely saved a run from scoring because there was no guarantee that I would have thrown him out even though I had a good jump on the ball. The bases remained loaded again for their RBI king. Gordie made a quick visit to the mound, probably reminding Ivan to stick with his forkball, which got him to groundout in his previous at bat. Ivan only needed three pitches to strike him out swinging to end yet another threat. We were still scoreless heading to the eighth.

The top of the eighth inning saw another 1-2-3 inning by the Saints as the Bulldog starter had now retired nine in a row. The same could not be said for Lawler, who seemed to be in a chaotic situation every time we turned around. The eighth was no different as the leadoff hitter stroked the first pitch to right field for a hit. After bunting the first pitch foul, the hitter was allowed to swing away, and he popped out to center. The crowd was silent except for one person who yelled out, "How did that work out for you, Coach?" It seems like fans think they know what is best when things don't go perfectly. The next player grounded a 2–2 pitch to Guzek at third. He went to second for one out, but Woody's throw to first went into the dugout. That gave the Bulldogs a runner in scoring position again. That brought up a player who had Lawler's number because he already had two hits on the night. He hit a ball high and deep to right that was caught just shy of the warning track by Sammy to end the inning. It was not an easy play since this was the first night game we played all year. We headed to the ninth with the score still 0–0.

I led off the top of the ninth with the same mantra as when we trailed the Golden Tornados several days ago: "Just get on base." I tried to bunt my way on but fouled it off. The pitcher then fell behind in the count 3–1. I hit a rocket to left for only our third hit of the night. That hit sent their coach to the mound to possibly discuss their defense against a bunt or steal. As play resumed, the pitcher threw over to first, and I was in easily. Rydberg chopped a ball to third, and that was just as effective as a sacrifice bunt because I scampered into second. Paprockas fouled off a bunt for a hit and later struck out. They issued an intentional walk to Lawler, who was replaced with the courtesy runner John Mika. That brought up our cleanup hitter, who was hitless in his last seven plate appearances but had the key hit in our come-from-behind victory over Geneva.

Dave DeHaan came to CSF, like many of his teammates, because he loved the way the coaching staff made him feel. He had a little extra motivation to stay near his home in Tinley Park because his mother had just given birth to a baby boy when he was looking at colleges. His grandparents, parents, and baby brother were here to see his next at bat. Dave was used to pressure-packed at bats early in his career in Joliet. His first college at bat in fall ball came against a hard-throwing transfer from Texas A&M. Dave loved the intensity of the moment, and this was another one of those moments. He hit a bounding ball into left field, and I was off with the crack of the bat since there were two outs and a runner behind me. The left fielder charged as Coach Delgado waved me home. The throw came to the plate as I dived to the outer half with the help of Guzek's coaching. The tag came down, and the plate umpire threw up his right arm in a fist to indicate that I was out. I threw my arms up in disbelief trying to petition the umpire, but my opinion was not taken into consideration. That was the second time of the game that they ended the inning by cutting down a runner at the plate. We headed to the bottom of the ninth, scoreless. I was disappointed that I was not fast enough to give us a lead that could catapult us into the championship game.

The bottom of the ninth started with a dreaded leadoff walk. He was advanced to second on a well-executed bunt fielded by DeHaan, who threw to Woody covering first. The winning run was now in scoring position. Chad Capista and Ed Young started to get loose in the pen as Ivan hit the next batter with a pitch on a 2–2 count. Coach decided to use a visit to talk with Lawler. Coach Gillespie was greeted by Ivan saying, "Don't even think of taking me out of this game. You will have to drag me off of this mound." Ivan was not being disrespectful; he just wanted Coach to know how much he wanted to stay in the game. The short visit from Gordie did not have the intended result as Ivan walked the hitter to load the bases and bring the winning run to within ninety feet. That again brought to the plate the offensive leader in almost every category. To make things worse, every defensive player was brought in to a position to where they could cut down the runner at the plate. A hard-hit ball would more than likely get past them. Strike one was a swing and a miss. The next pitch was a line drive to shallow center. Paprockas caught it and built some momentum for the throw home. Jones caught it in front of the plate on the second hop, but the runner only bluffed home since the cleanup hitter was next. More often than not, the cleanup hitter is one of the top hitters in the lineup, and that held true for Cumberland. He hit a ball past the pitcher, but Rydberg was there and stepped on second to send this ball game into extra innings.

Lawler was able to keep these hitters off-balance so well because he had complete confidence in his catcher, Bob Jones. He was confident that Bob would block any pitch that was in the dirt. This allowed Ivan to be more aggressive with his forkball and curveball. Some pitchers will make a mistake with a pitch and hang it for a hitter because they are afraid the ball could get away and runners would advance or even score. Bob's defense allowed all our pitchers to attack their game plan. Bob had learned a lot from his former roommate, Alex Fernandez, who graduated the previous year.

Guzek led off the top of the tenth with sharp single. He was lifted for a pinch runner since we had a onetime reentry rule. John Mika was now over at first. After a few failed bunt attempts, Woody hit a rocket right at the left fielder. Dan Samuilis waited patiently in the box as the pitcher made several pickoff attempts to first anticipating a steal attempt. Sammy fouled off several pitches before driving the ball to deep center field. The center fielder went back, back, back and caught the ball with his back to the wall. On any other day, that ball would have been gone, but today it was just a long out. Sammy was known for his power. He led the JV team as a freshman with seven home runs. In our junior year, he bailed me out of a base-running blunder by hitting a game-winning three-run home run. Jones then hit a ball down the right field line in foul ground near the bull pen. The right fielder was there for the play but whiffed on it, giving Bob another opportunity. Unfortunately, he tapped back to the pitcher to end the inning.

Lawler was still on mound for the bottom of the tenth. He had a quick inning. Only one man reached but was quickly erased on a 5-4-3 inning ending double play. The inning only took three pitches since every hitter hacked at the first offering. This is the exact person that I remembered meeting the summer after my senior year in high school. My legion team traveled to Racine to play Ivan's team. My teammates quickly learned that they had a player going to CSF as well; they called us the St. Francis connection. My buddies also teased me at the end of the game about how Ivan outplayed me. I was glad to be on his side now.

Their pitcher cruised through the top of the eleventh inning by striking me out. He then popped Rydberg up and then ended the inning when Paprockas dribbled back to the mound. If Ivan was going to lead off the next inning, he would have to shut the Bulldogs down again.

This would not be easy since the man leading off had been on base three times already. He made it a fourth when he hit a slow roller that Rydberg mishandled. The next player attempted to sacrifice bunt on the first pitch. He pushed it toward the second basemen, and as Ivan came off the mound, he slipped down on to all fours. Rain had made the field slick, and this fact helped every runner to be safe since Ivan could not regain his footing. The following hitter fouled a bunt back on the first pitch with Dave DeHaan only thirty-five feet away. That changed their strategy, so he swung away to make it 0–2. He struck out on the next pitch when he missed the bunt. The next hitter bounded a ball to third, and Guzek went to second for one, but that was the only out we got. Runners were at first and third with two outs and another opportunity for their most prolific RBI man. Lawler continued to have his number as he grounded out to second base. He was 0–5 and stranded eleven base runners on the night. I am sure the pressure of his team counting on him and failing was very difficult. Yet another crisis was avoided. How many times would a Lawler be able to walk this tightrope?

For the second inning in a row, we sent three men to the plate, and they were set down in order. A quick turnaround for Lawler, who faced the cleanup hitter to start the inning. He roped a sharp single past a diving Guzek. They then executed a perfect bunt to the right side to put the winning run at second with only one out. Not a single fan was sitting down. Each one was pacing back and forth in nervous anticipation. The next hitter had two hits on the night but struck out on a ball in on his hands. The following man hit a ball in the air to right, which sliced away from Sammy, who had a long run. He could not get there, but the wind pushed it about a foot foul. The next pitch was a ball in the dirt blocked by Jones out in front of the plate. The runner took off for third, but Jones recovered quickly and threw a bullet to third for the final out of the inning. Experts believe you should not make the first or last out of the inning at third since you are already in scoring position. Our team was relieved that their base runner ignored this guideline. We welcomed this quick out. Lawler continued to wiggle his way out of jams; how much more magic could he possibly have left?

Their pitcher faced the bottom of our order to start the thirteenth inning. What an amazing feat to have two starting pitchers dueling this late in the ball game. The starter was still in and seemed to be on cruise control. Sammy quickly bounced out to second. Bob Jones attempted another bunt for a base hit but was unsuccessful. He stayed alive by fouling off four pitches in a row before he looped a ball into right for a hit. Gordie decided to let him run for himself this time. Bob had such good speed that in high school, he was actually a running back. I looked to bunt, but the first three pitches to me were balls. I decided to take the next two pitches for strikes. I struck out again on a ball that I believed was ball four. Rydberg got behind in the count 0–2 but was able to even count. Rydberg noticed that the pitcher had retired him a few times in the game by staying on the outside part of the plate. He decided to crowd the plate and got the exact pitch that he anticipated. Most pitchers assumed that this five-foot-eight-inch shortstop did not have much power. The next pitch was up and away, so Rydberg went with the pitch and drove it deep to right. This showed his power to all fields. The right fielder got on his horse and reached up, trying to make a play like Willie Mays, but it tipped off the end of his outstretched glove. This right fielder was the same player that had left so many runners stranded offensively. Talk about a player having a bad day. Jones headed for home for the first run of the night. Rydberg stood on second as a valuable insurance run. On the next pitch, Rydberg tried to block the view of the ball when Paprockas grounded to third, but he fielded it and easily threw him out at first, but the damage was done. We headed to the bottom of the thirteenth clinging to a one-run lead.

Lawler headed out to the mound again even though he had thrown 187 pitches entering the inning. This was actually the second-highest total for Ivan. He threw 213 pitches in a 12-inning loss to Wisconsin, Oshkosh, as a freshman. He seemed to be more energized with a one-run lead and struck out the first two hitters for a total of nine. The next hitter popped up, and Lawler started jumping up and down, celebrating even before our shortstop squeezed it. This was the first time that anyone on the team would go near or even talk to him. When a pitcher is in a zone, it is customary to leave him alone. We were not going to break the code of superstition at this critical point in the year. We took the opportunity to mob Ivan because the game was over and we were headed to the championship game.

It was one of Lawler's quickest innings of the night. The final score was 1–0. Ivan Lawler was named the player of the game by outdueling the opposing pitcher. He even exceeded Ochman's performance by shutting them out for thirteen innings instead of just nine. He threw a total of 196 pitches. The Saints committed three errors for the first time since the spring trip, but luckily, the result was not the same. I was also off the hook because our clean uniforms were on the winning side.

Only two teams remained, Southeastern Oklahoma and us. The tournament directors confirmed that the game was moved up to two o'clock because of the predicted rain. The Savages would have to win two games to be crowned champions, but we only needed to win once. None of us dared talk about the next game. There was a quiet confidence about what needed to be done. We knew that talking about it was pointless; only our performance could get us to our common goal.

Chapter 14

Game 5 — Saints vs. Savages: the Rematch

T he Savages wore their white uniforms with navy-blue pinstripes, numbers, and letters. We continued to wear the exact same uniform for the fifth game in a row and quite possibly the entire playoffs. The only change to their lineup was a different lefty starting pitcher. Our lineup was the same as our last game with the exception of Samuilis becoming the designated hitter for starting pitcher Paul Chovanec while Ivan Lawler played right field. Many people were surprised that Ivan could even pick his arm up after his heroic effort on the mound the night before. His experience and toughness earned him the spot in right field. Chovy had been experiencing some shoulder issues in his last few games but nothing that would keep him from going after his fourteenth win and a national championship. Truth be told, this was the first time he picked up a ball since his last start. He also loaded up on Advil before the game.

The weather was better than the day before, but still overcast with a little more sun fighting through the clouds. The game was moved up to two o'clock with the chance of showers in the evening. The slightly warmer weather made it a perfect day for players, but not ideal for spectators. Louise was back for another game and was joined by our sister Terri and her husband, Mike. Of course, nothing could keep my parents away from Sec Taylor Stadium today. The wind was howling in during the pregame announcement of the line-ups. It would be a good day to utilize our speed and play some "small ball." Coach Gillespie's wife, Joan, was chosen to sing the national anthem. The team was excited because we did not lose a game all year long when she was singing at the game. We got the first offensive opportunity since we were the visitors.

Steve Ochman got a little retribution by visiting Paul Chovanec as he warmed up in the bull pen. He subtly said, "Boy, you were right, these guys are big." Chovy laughed because he knew exactly what Steve was doing. Ochman took it a step further and said, "Don't worry, if we lose, I am pitching next, and I showed that I can handle them." Paul finished up his work with a big smile on his face. He had the perfect balance of being relaxed and focused.

Dave Rydberg grounded out to second on the first pitch of the game. Paprockas gave us our first base runner when he worked the count to full and then took a base on balls. He advanced all the way to third when Ivan Lawler singled up the middle on a 2–2 pitch. The Saints again looked to take an early lead. Paprockas scampered home when Dave DeHaan swung and missed at a pitch in the dirt that eluded the catcher to the backstop. Ivan was stranded at second when DeHaan struck out and Guzek grounded to first for an unassisted putout. We hoped the early lead would hold up. Getting an early lead is just what every team wants, especially when the stakes are so high. We hoped it would increase the pressure on our opponent.

We felt confident with a lead and Paul Chovanec on the mound. Earlier in the year, he tossed a no-hitter, and he was in position to win his fourteenth game, which only four other players in NAIA history were able to accomplish. He also had a bet with Lawler that he would have more strikeouts for the year, and he trailed by seven. He cut that down to six by striking out the leadoff man looking. He fell behind in the count to the next hitter but induced a weak grounder to short. The final out of the inning came on a ball that was sliced down the left field line. I had a long run but was able to track it down. Three up and three down was the perfect way for us to start the ball game.

The Savages responded with their own 1-2-3 inning, which put Chovy right back on the mound with little rest. The bottom of the second started with an infield hit. Rydberg made a heroic attempt on a ball in the hole, but the throw got away from DeHaan. There was no error on the play because Jones was backing up. The next hitter walked to put the tying run in scoring position. Both runners moved up to second and third after a passed ball on Jones. Chovy struck out the next batter for the first out of the inning. The critical play of the inning came when Chovy caught the base runner at third sleeping and picked him off with a perfect throw to Guzek. The runner would have scored when the next pitch was rapped on the ground to second. Woody mishandled it, and the runners were safe at first and third. This was a dangerous position because many teams run a gimmick play with two outs and runners on the corners. However, the Savages did not, and the threat ended with a fly out to Paprockas in center.

The top of the third started harmlessly when I bounced out to first base. Rydberg then walked on four straight balls. Dave rarely swung at bad pitches, which was apparent by his 0.490 batting average when he was at Harlem High School in Rockford. He should have been eliminated when the lefty pitcher caught him leaning toward second, but Rydberg took off and ended up at third when the throw sailed over the first baseman's head and into the bull pen. Their coach came out to the mound for a short visit and decided to bring the infield in to medium depth. The infield depth couldn't prevent Rydberg from scoring when Paprockas bounced to second for out number two. Lawler singled and then surprised everyone by stealing second. Ivan was stranded when DeHaan struck out. We felt more in control when we increased our lead to 2–0, but there was still a long way to go in this ball game.

Both pitchers retired the side in order in the bottom of the third and the top of the fourth. The Savages looked to cut the lead in the bottom half of the fourth. Chovy got the first out of the inning by covering first on a ball hit to DeHaan in the hole. The cleanup hitter then doubled down the left field line. He advanced to third when the teammate who followed hit a deep fly ball to right. He was now only ninety feet away from cutting the lead in half. Runners in scoring position was not something that rattled Paul. He was able to focus his attention and energy on the batter in front of him. Chovy inched closer to Lawler's strikeout total when he struck out the batter for the second time, inning over.

Bob Jones led off the top of the fifth with a single and took an extra base on an error. John Mika came in as his courtesy runner. I received a high five from everyone in the dugout when I successfully sacrificed him over to third. We had a runner at third with one out and the top of our lineup coming to the plate. Rydberg hit a shot, but it was right at the third basemen, so Mika stayed put. Paprockas drove in his second run of the day on an infield single with two outs. Gordie would always tease us that two out RBIs could get us into heaven, and with a three-run lead, I was feeling closer than ever before. The interesting part of the play was that the third basemen was in to guard against all his bunt attempts. This dramatically cut down on his range, so the shortstop had to field the ball deep in the hole. If the third basemen was in his normal position, he would have easily thrown Kerry out. This was a great example about how playing all phases of the game can influence the game in your favor later on. The inning ended when Lawler struck out swinging.

The Savages proved in the bottom half of the fifth that they would not give up easily on their quest for a national title. The lead-off man singled to center on the first pitch. He stole second on a botched hit-and-run where the batter struck out. Chovy then walked the nine hitter to role the lineup over. Two on and one out for the top of the order. The leadoff hitter looped a single to right to drive in the first run for the Savages. They cut the lead to 3–1 and had runners on the corners with still only one out. It appeared that a big inning was brewing for the Savages. Action started again in our bull pen since the heart of the order was due up, but Gordie stuck with his senior captain, who was a huge reason why we made it this far. Coach rarely used relief pitchers during the season; he trusted and challenged his starters to finish their work.

The next thing I knew, I was streaking toward the left center field gap. I left my feet and dove as far as I could to make the catch of my life. I had the good sense to jump up and fire a strike to my relay man, VanderWoude, who doubled the trail runner off first. The runner planned on scoring on the shot and had rounded second before seeing me catch it. The runner scored from third before we got the unconventional double play to make the score 3–2. We escaped the inning with only allowing two runs. If I had not made this catch, the score would have been tied and the go ahead run would have been at second with only one out. As I ran to the dugout, I couldn't help but think of my diving catch playing "silo ball" as a child. I had spent hours and hours on something that now seemed to be training me for this one specific moment in time. I made the exact same catch in my childhood, and now it felt like my destiny. I had prepared my whole life for that one play. I hoped it would be enough to catapult us to a national championship. The excitement that I felt at that moment was inching closer to the feeling I had when I saved the Cubs in the World Series.

Offensively, we went quietly in the top of the sixth. That put Paul Chovanec right back on the mound with little rest. Chovy retired the first two of the inning on groundouts. Every Saints fan in the stadium held their collective breath when the next lefty hitter went the other way to deep left. Fortunately for us, the wind had shifted and forced the ball beyond the foul pole before it left the yard. Otherwise, we would have been tied up. Paul walked him on the next pitch. The inning ended when the next batter struck out for his third time and threw his bat and helmet down in disgust. This was entertaining to our team because Coach Gillespie always emphasized a different type of behavior. We were expected to carry ourselves with class at all times even when things were going poorly. He also believed that cooler heads would prevail when it was crunch time. Gordie loved to talk about how you could not tell what the score was when Barry Sanders and Walter Payton played because they acted the same way all the time. They brought stability to their team, and that was exactly what he wanted from us.

For the second inning in a row, Paul Chovanec did not have much of a break because we went down in order to start the seventh. Action started in our bull pen when Chovy walked the opposing catcher with one out. Their courtesy runner stole second to move into scoring position. The go-ahead run was put on first base when Chovy again walked the nine hitter. The runners were at first and second with only one out, while we clung to a one-run lead. It felt as if the Savages had scoring opportunities every inning, but Paul was able get even tougher in those moments, but we wondered how much he had left in his sore shoulder. I hoped for another ground ball since our infield had turned so many double plays. The crisis was over when the next two players popped out on the infield. We were six defensive outs away from College of St. Francis's first ever national championship. Counting down the outs went against the superstitious nature of baseball enthusiasts, but it never prevents us from doing it.

Chovy was our closer the previous two seasons and was only twenty-six appearances shy of holding the career record at CSF. We even nicknamed him "Dibble" because he reminded us of the closer for the Cincinnati Reds at the time. Even though, I would guess that Rob Dibble did not have the chicken legs that Paul did. I had never seen such a big guy with such skinny legs. Paul could handle the grief we gave him for it because he loved to dish it out. Early in his career as our closer, he got an earful from Gordie about how he should close out a game. Paul gave up a big hit to a batter on a chan-geup, which was Paul's third best pitch. Gordie yelled, "I hired you to knock down poles!" His message was clear that from now on, if he is in doubt, challenge the hitter with his best pitch, the cut fastball.

Before the season started, he sat down with Coach to discuss the possibility of becoming a starter. Gordie agreed to give him an opportunity in Texas. Paul pitched with a bit of a chip on his shoul-der because he had something to prove. He knew that there was a good chance that he would be relegated back to the bull pen if he had one bad start. He rewarded himself, Gordie, and the team by being undefeated up to this point.

Coach Gillespie was clearly a master motivator because several players in the lineup had something to prove. Bob Jones did not see much time before this year because he was stuck behind our star catcher, Alex Fernandez. He wanted to show he could perform at the standard that had been set at that position. Matt Sisson was also catching the majority of the time until he was injured several weeks ago. Bob wanted to show that he deserved to catch each game. Dan Samuilis had split time at first base for the last two seasons and wanted to establish himself as a big part of the lineup. He even changed positions to make that possible. Kerry Paprockus was initially overlooked as a freshman and spent that entire campaign on the junior varsity team. He wanted to show that he was as good as the other "super sophomores." He had to prove himself again this year because he knew the coaches thought highly of John Mika. He had a previous rivalry with John when their schools, Montini Catholic and Driscoll Catholic, played each other. I shared a kinship with these gentlemen because it felt like we had to try just a little bit harder. Everyone on the team worked hard, but there was more on the line for all of us. Desire was our great equalizer, and the team benefited from it. The best part was what we all became because of that determination.

The top of the eighth started off promising with a leadoff single, but it evaporated quickly when Rydberg was caught trying to steal and the next two players struck out when the closer of the Savages came into the game. The same could not be said for the Savages in the bottom half of the inning. Chovy had to face the heart of their order. The three hitter lined a single to center to get things going. Gordie again strolled out to the mound to discuss different scenarios. The opposing coach elected to let his cleanup hitter swing away instead of sacrificing. Chovy responded with a critical strikeout. The next batter hit a laser beam to right field for a sharp single, and the lead runner held at second. For the third consecutive inning, the Savages were threatening. The sixth hitter completed his day with a "golden sombrero," meaning he struck out for the fourth time. However, the situation became more complicated when Chovy walked the next man on four straight pitches. The go-ahead run was now in scoring position.

My father would not stand next to anyone because he felt like it gave us better luck. He told me that there were plenty of fans using every superstitious routine that they could think of to guide us through the next few outs. Everything was on the line in this critical situation. Could Chovy remain undefeated? Could he pass Lawler in strikeouts? Could we hold on for the national title? The first pitch was swung on and missed. Pitch number two was a ball outside. It was followed by a swing and a miss for strike two. The next pitch froze the hitter on the inside corner for Chovanec's eighth K of the game. He passed Lawler's mark and was only three defensive outs away from an unblemished record and a national championship.

Their closer started the ninth with his third consecutive strike-out. Guzek then took an inside-out swing and fisted a ball into right for a single. He was lifted for a pinch runner, John Mika. Late in the count, Mika stole second; this came immediately after a pitchout on the previous pitch. Two pitches later, Woody drew a base on balls. A wild pitch to Sammy moved both runners into scoring position. The infield moved in to the infield grass so they could cut down the runner at the plate. The closer's control left him again as he walked Samuilis to load the bases. Sammy later told me that his main goal in his final at bat was to avoid the "hat trick," striking out three times. Bob Jones, who had come up with some key hits, was now standing in the box. He grinded out the at bat until he was able to hit a sacrifice fly to add on an insurance run and make it 4–2 Saints. One extra run may not seem like much, but in the world of baseball, it can make all the difference.

Brian Olsen came in to pinch-hit for me. Of course, I was disappointed that I wouldn't be taking possibly the last at bat of my career, but I thought about it from his perspective. This was only his second opportunity of the World Series. He was the player not in the lineup when Gordie penciled me in all five games. Brian was the ultimate team player because he waited patiently for his chance and didn't complain in the meantime. Unfortunately, he stranded the two runners when he struck out looking.

Chovy returned to the mound in the ninth, going for another complete game victory. Brian Guzek and I reentered the ball game for defensive purposes. Chovy started the inning with the dreaded leadoff walk to the nine hitter yet again. The tying run came to the plate with no one out. There was not a single fan who was able to sit in their seat at this point in the game. They were all pacing back and forth trying to influence the outcome for their team. The leadoff man lifted a deep high fly to left that I was able to camp under, for out number one. The twitch in my eye had vanished, and I hoped that was a sign that the end was near. The two hitter grounded the ball to Guzek, who threw to VanderWoude at second for one; he threw to first, but it was not in time to double up the speedy runner. Chovy walked the three hitter to create high drama in Des Moines. With two outs, a double could easily score the runner from first and tie the game. This was exactly why the insurance run was so necessary. The complexion of the game was entirely different now.

The four hitter strode to the plate representing the winning run. The cleanup hitter had eleven home runs on the year, and the wind was now blowing out. He also hit a moon shot home run against us to defeat us on the spring trip. The game could be over with one swing of the bat. That would create a winner-takes-all scenario the next day. Chovy, Sammy, Ivan, and I were all in Anderson, Indiana, two years ago when the wheels fell off. I hoped our leadership could prevent an identical outcome.

Here was the call from the radio voice of Scott Slocum on WJOL: "It's in the air. It's in the air. That could do it. VanderWoude on the outfield grass, he has it. The Saints win the national championship. The College of St. Francis wins the 1993 NAIA World Series. The school's first ever national championship. There is a mob out on the infield. The Saints are going crazy, you gotta love it, folks."

We had done it, and all our dreams came true. As predicted, Rydberg tackled VanderWoude after the final out. I jumped on top of both of them as everyone else swarmed Chovy near the mound. Maybe the most amazing statistic from the year was that we won thirty-eight of our last thirty-nine games. A stark contrast from the 3-13-2 start. Proving once again that it matters not how you start but how you finish. Not bad for a group of guys who had the third-lowest batting average in school history.

I am leading the charge to hug Coach Gillespie. His
extended arms indicate that he was ready for me.

I gave way so my teammates could
congratulate the coaches as well.

Chapter 15

Postgame

T he mob on the field is what you will see after every championship. Grown men were hugging, jumping around, giving high
fives, and some were even crying with joy. It appeared as if we had
transformed into little children again with the enthusiasm of our celebration. A bond was formed over that year, and it was solidified into
a brotherhood when the final out was made. From this point on, no
matter what life would bring at us, we were champions. Years could
pass, but that bond would connect us forever; no matter how much
time passed, we could return to that moment in an instant. When
we finished greeting every teammate near the mound, I led the team
over to the coaching staff in front of the dugout. I will never forget
being the first player to hug Gordie after the game. The whole team
then engulfed the entire coaching staff.

The celebration would continue, but it was time for the awards
ceremony. The players and coaches of Southeastern Oklahoma were
called up as individuals to receive their second-place plaques. A
plaque was also given to Kerry Paprockas for driving in the winning
run in the championship game. It was a perfect bookend for him
since he drove in the winning run in both the first and last game
of the World Series. Ivan Lawler was named the tournament Most
Valuable Player. Adam VanderWoude won the Charles Berry Hustle
award. Paul Chovanec, Bob Jones, Ivan Lawler, and Dave Rydberg

made the all-tournament team from our squad. Paul Chovanec also solidified his spot as the NAIA Player of the Year.

We set a new record with the most double plays turned at the World Series. Our pitchers also set a new standard for the fewest runs allowed. It eclipsed a mark set by Lewis University during the years that Coach Gillespie was there.

The championship trophy and banner were presented to Gordie, and the entire team took a picture with those items in front of the pitcher's mound. The trophy was made of wood and was nearly four feet tall. The base was in the shape of home plate, while the center column looked like a bat being carved out of a tree. Two more columns had small placards which were engraved with the winning school and the year. Many of us made sure we got a picture with it.

The entire team was also called up as individuals to receive our national championship plaques. The experience was so surreal that it is hard to remember everything that transpired. We spent close to an hour milling about, talking to one another, friends, and family. The common theme among us was how sad we were that the season was now over. We all remarked at how everyone played an important role and recognized that it was a total team effort. It seemed like there was a different hero every game.

I was most impressed by the players who did not get an opportunity to play during the World Series. They were competitors just like the rest of us and wanted a chance to help us win as well. They did not complain when Gordie did not put them into the game. Instead, they swallowed their pride and cheered on their teammates. At no point did anyone sulk. They were off the bench and engaged in the game on every pitch. I admired those players the most because it could have easily been me in their position. I knew how they felt because I spent the previous three seasons in their position. I truly believe the outcome would have been different if we had any dissension on the team at all. It was a sign of just how special our group was that nobody cared who got the credit as long as we won. That team spirit was a huge factor in our success. We realized that we needed one another to accomplish our goal.

It was euphoric for many reasons. Everything that we experienced on our journey was worth it. Suddenly, the early-morning practices did not seem so early; the long practices did not seem so long. Realizing that the little details our coaches preached all those years made all the difference in those close games. It was even more rewarding because we were not the most talented group. It was quite possible that this was the reason we won. We had to try harder, work harder, and grow closer as a unit to pull off such a lofty goal. We were not the most talented team St. Francis ever had, but we *could* claim that we were the best *team.*

We were overjoyed by the result, but we realized that our time together was nearly over. Some of us would never play the sport that we loved again. When you love something so much you never want it to end, you soak up as much as you could in those remaining moments. The sorrow involved everything that revolved around this great game. We would miss the competitiveness that comes out when being thrust into difficult situations, the excitement of the unknown that each game naturally brings. The sights and sounds of baseball are unlike any other sport. Smelling the fresh-cut grass as you chew sunflower seeds while the crack of the bat rings in your ear is something special. Seeing an unusual play for the first time can make you understand the endless possibilities of the unexpected.

I was sure that I would simply miss my teammates, the bond that we created formed by the most mundane things. It could have been by giving a high five after a job well done. Sometimes it would be when we would console one another with a pat on the back after a tough loss or an individual mistake. The friendships grew as stories were shared on the bench or in the dorms. The flashes of the smiles and laughter shared during the chill of March and the warmth of May come rushing back as if it happened in an instant. I wanted to freeze time and stay in this euphoria forever. In my heart, I knew it would always be with me, but in my brain, I knew it would fade with time.

Dave Laketa spent the last half inning on the field anticipating the victory. He interviewed the coaches and a large number of players. When Dave asked Paul Chovanec how his shoulder felt, he responded, "I didn't have my good stuff today because of my shoulder, so I had to throw with my heart instead." This really typified who we were as a team. We had a lot of heart. Sports can be a test of your resiliency. I was so proud that no one gave up on our dream when we got off to such a poor start in Texas.

One of my friends who could not be at the game said he listened to the whole game in Joliet and loved my postgame interview. I was surprised that I could even put my elation into words. I also thought of my high school coach who told me he staked his reputation on me. I told my dad to call him and let him know that I held up my end of the bargain. I was pretty sure that Gordie would take another player like me and Coach Shield's reputation was still in good standing with Gordie.

I don't remember the trip back to the hotel, but I remember Coach Gillespie's final instructions in the lobby. He told us to get showered and packed and be back in the lobby in forty-five minutes. The team dispersed and went to their rooms as instructed. Within a few minutes, the phone rang, and I answered it. It was Coach Gillespie. I recognized his voice immediately, and he recognized mine. He got very stern with me and said, "Paul Babcock, you are a senior captain. Can you explain to me why an old man like me is down here loading the bus up by myself?"

I started to stammer, "C-C-C-Coach, I thought you told us to be down there in forty-five minutes. I am so sorry."

He started to laugh and said, "Paul, I'm just teasing you. I wanted you to know that, that was the greatest catch I have ever seen and it is the reason we won the national championship today."

I was stunned. My head swelled to twice its size, and my heart almost burst with pride. I managed to squeak out a meager "Thanks, Coach, I appreciate it."

As I hung up the phone, my eyes welled up with tears because I came to the realization that I accomplished my dream of my team winning Gordie a national championship at St. Francis. Every extra thing that I did to prepare was worth it. There were so many clear lessons that I learned from my journey. The first was that I will never have regrets when I give it all I possibly can. I also learned that hard work can pay off, especially when I never ever give up. It was apparent to me that focusing on the team first brought me more happiness than I could ever get by myself. The total team effort is the only way anything worthwhile can be accomplished, and when I love the person next to me, we will do anything for each other. My advice to any young person would be simple: never ever, ever give up, and all great success stories start with someone saying "You can't do it."

It still felt like we were in a dreamland as we packed up the bus and my truck. The final object that needed to be packed was the championship trophy. Gordie brought it over to my truck and set on top of the luggage. Even though it looked perfect, I was stunned again. I could not comprehend the significance of this moment. I was carrying back the symbol of what I had been chasing for all these years. As we rolled down the road, I would glance in the rearview mirror and see it resting where it belonged. I could not help but see the irony. The very thing that I was always going after was now behind me but would always be riding with me.

We stopped for dinner on the way back to Joliet, appropriately nicknamed "City of Champions." Mike Kieltyka and John Dagres made the four-and-a-half-hour trek out to Des Moines to witness our crowning achievement. They were my teammates in football freshman year, and we stayed close. They followed us to the restaurant and seemed just as happy as the rest of us. It meant a lot to me that they could share in this moment. Other friends and family showed up, and we had one last meal together. It helped me realize that so many people played a role in our success. Each one of us was impacted in different ways on our journey to the same destination. The energy was phenomenal, and no one could stop from smiling. Gordie / St. Francis was so happy that he/they picked up the tab for anyone there who cheered for the Saints. I am certain that there was a deep satisfaction for Gordie, who had been to the World Series several times with CSF but had come up short until now.

The rest of the ride home was a blur. I am sure Jason King and I never shut up about what had just transpired. Before I knew it, we were pulling into the parking lot of our recreation center on campus. I heard Jason say, "Hey, look at that." On the windows of the athletic facility, I saw three posters in the shape of players. One was crouched as a catcher with the name Jones on the back. The two others were of players swinging a bat. One jersey said DeHaan, and the other said Babcock. A lump formed in my throat as I read the caption above my figure: "The only thing better than a *dream* is when it becomes *reality.*"

I love this picture because you can see how much I admire Coach Gillespie. It didn't hurt that we were national champions.

Paul Babcock and Dave DeHaan holding
the championship trophy

The whole team with the trophy and championship banner

This was on the rec. center when we returned to campus. I couldn't laminate the quote, but I could laminate this. This resides in my garage to this day.

Every member of "the team" received this championship ring.

About the Author

Paul Babcock became a teacher and coach because he wanted to make an impact on people like the one Coach Gillespie made on him. He continues to spread Coach Gillespie's message on leadership through keynote speeches and presentations at coaches' clinics. Fortunately, he met his best friend while he was at the College of St. Francis and is still married to her with four children. He has continued to conquer his goals by completing an ironman triathlon and developing an annual family sprint triathlon on his parents' farm. He continued his methodical approach to accomplishing his goals by completing his one millionth pushup on his 40th birthday. It took thirteen years of dedication and determination. Life continues to teach him that most things are possible if you are willing to work harder than everyone else.

Contact Paul for speaking engagements at babcockpaul711@gmail.com

Lightning Source UK Ltd.
Milton Keynes UK
UKHW022258130619
344361UK00004B/21/P

9 781644 628119